John Fuller

SELECTED POEMS
1954–1982

JOHN FULLER

Selected Poems

1954 to 1982

SECKER & WARBURG
LONDON

First published in England 1985 by
Martin Secker & Warburg Limited
54 Poland Street, London W1V 3DF

Copyright © John Fuller 1985

British Library Cataloguing in Publication Data

Fuller, John, *1937–*
    Selected poems 1954 to 1982.
    I. Title
    821'.914   PR6054.U43

    ISBN 0–436–16754–9

Typeset by Inforum Ltd, Portsmouth
Printed in Great Britain by
Redwood Burn Ltd, Trowbridge

ACKNOWLEDGEMENTS

Fairground Music and *The Tree that Walked* were published by Chatto and Windus; *Cannibals and Missionaries, Epistles to Several Persons, The Mountain in the Sea, Lies and Secrets, The Illusionists* and *The Beautiful Inventions* were published by Secker and Warburg; and *Waiting for the Music* was published by the Salamander Press.

CONTENTS

FAIRY TALE

Blushing, she fled: no one was on her side.
She could not bear the whistle and the slap,
The fustian prospect of a farmer's lap.
Her father moped. Her sisters swore. She cried,
Dreamed of the Prince, neglected all her tasks
And now had run away, but not for long:
The wood was frightful as a wig, as wrong
As her own hearth. Soon she returned, through masks
Of mist. Her heart jumped at the stir that took
Her eye: the royal hounds sagged in the porch,
Their tongues like shoehorns. Someone waved a torch.
Hardly believing, breathless, she ran to look –
But worse than all the sniggers of the wood,
The waiting Prince was ugly, pale and good.

A KISS IN GALLOWAY

Sea, buttoned snails and catapulted gulls,
Small world turned over and over on itself:
China and crystal on the cottage shelf,
The fire-reflecting brass and stranded hulls
In pale landscapes, steaming articles
For walking in the waves draped round the hearth
Like priestly robes. Coming back up the path
With beer, you make that gesture which annuls
Once more what gracelessness our history has,
And in the twilight where the butterfly
Unfolds her carpet beauty, slowly, as slow
As too-rich dew creeps on dead summer's grasses,
We seal our fatal promise to defy
That we may be delivered into woe.

THE AEGEAN

Chickens on board, eyes blinking, trussed alive,
The siren's tongue of steam, a restless night,
White columns in the moon's decaying light,
Travellers humped in bags, awake; at five
The sailors uncoil ropes and we arrive
At yet another island. People cough.
The sleeping harbour sends its small boats off.
The anchor does a belly-flopping dive.

O night! O moon! Staring and staring, we
Might lie forever on this parting wake:
Call up the waves and wind, stir us and make
Us crumble like those cities, stunned, until,
Another ruin on the endless sea
Our ship steams through, our love stands ever still.

THE STATUE

Your buttonholes for eyes, your solemn face,
The golden hair against your sleeping back:
This is no other time, no other place,
A moment certain as the almanac,
Vivid as weather, quiet as the deep,
As innocent as hands that curl in sleep.

For dreams disguise our wish to be awake
With bells, lagoons and squalls of tinsel trees.
In dreams you are not cruel, yet can't fake
An understanding of your cruelties.
Later, we're on the road: our object is
To judge a dead art's possibilities.

The radiator choked with butterflies,
We reach the city in a thumbed-down car
And I discover that the staring eyes
And cool lips of the promised statue are,
Though fabulous, immortalised in stone,
Less rare and calm and perfect than your own.

For, in the camera's illusion, he
Preserved a moment from a laughing past,
A consolation for inconstancy,
Carefree, amorous, dynamic, vast,
Making a message on a mantelpiece,
A famous face sent by a friend from Greece.

But when we view the postcard subject fresh,
Gazing from curls to reconstructed toes,
Gone is the gentle and the human flesh,
Slyly dramatic in a talking pose:
Instead I see, and think I understand
The broken smile, whips in the missing hand.

BAND MUSIC

Cows! Cows! With ears like mouths of telephones!
They creak towards him with their heads thrust out,
So baby wauls among the cabbages
Till Betty runs to kiss his quivering pout
And lumping Ernest takes a stick and stones
To drive them off, cursing their ravages.

'Hush, child,' she whispers, rocking. 'There, there then!
Watch Ernest. Clever Ernest. Nasty cows.'
Inside the cottage from a dusty box
Thumps martial music. Flowers on Betty's blouse
Grow out in lines like cabbages while men
In gold braid blow among the hollyhocks.

FAIRGROUND MUSIC

Dispirited, the Sun of Persia
And his hordes return
To distance and to longing.
Haggard painted horses
Glossy with angry curls
Express his orbit;
Paper axles spin and burn
With proper fury.
But flowered Babylon
Amid the smiling pipes,
Amid the gentle drum,
Is troubled still
By whirring scythes and music,
Sleeping, is oppressed
By alien beards and tents.
Rough Cyrus roars
For talismans and charts;
The whole collision
Is of smarting red and green
Thick with the smoking blood.
The fall of Babylon!
A mercenary there
Rummaged in slub and carcase
For some prize or toy
And found a thing that troubled
Cyrus so, he wept, and saw
Within the tinkling of
A turning box,
Shore-fighters, crabs,
Girl-scorpions,
Splashing in weightless
Liquid gold about the rocks.

EDWARDIAN CHRISTMAS

Father's opinion of savages
And dogs, a gay Bloomsbury epigram:
'The brutes may possibly have souls,' he says,
'But reason, no. Nevertheless, I am
Prepared not to extend this to my spouse
And children.' This demands a careful pity:
Poor Father! Whooping and romping in their house,
A holiday from ruin in the City.
His wit falls flat, his tie just will not tie.
The dog's in chains, the reasonable books
Grazed by his children as they learn to fly.
He takes his dear wife's arm (his hands grow hooks).
Pirates and pudding! Come, such cruelty!

His beard is branching like a burning tree.

WHITE QUEEN

Who has a feeling she will come one day,
No pretty, silly girl, nor beautiful
Like Marlowe's Spirit, unapproachable,
But gray, gray, gray from being shut away?

For this is what the poets will not say:
'Helen grew paler and was old, I fear,
(Sixty at Troy's loud fall) and for a year
Was seen by no one, wandering fat and gray.'

In her appearance all will have their say.
Movements of flesh about eternal needs
Promote the spectacle of Helen's deeds
In the mind's eye at least, but in what way?

What figure scampers as this verse begins,
Ashen and wailing, scattering veils and pins?

ESSAY ON SPENSER

Clownish without his armour, he
Clamped down his umbriere. His sword
Knocking against the trees, men fell
About him, headless, twitching. His
Thick heart jumping, he plunged through
The steaming wood until against
His Lady's Tower, sword down, he gasped
The rune to move the man-high stone
That blocked her keeping, up again
He raced the spiral shaft and beat
In rage the spellbound oak. And died.
For a splintered mirror spoilt her plan
To save him from the littered plain,
And all that night fell frogs and rain.

IN A RAILWAY COMPARTMENT

Oxford to London, 1884:
Against the crimson arm-rest leaned a girl
Of ten, holding a muff, twisting a curl,
Drumming her heels in boredom on the floor
Until a white-haired gentleman who saw
She hated travelling produced a case
Of puzzles: 'Seven Germans run a race . . .
Unwind this maze, escape the lion's paw . . .
The princess must be lowered by her hair . . .'
The train entered a tunnel, shrieking, all
The lights went out and when he took her hand
She was the princess in the tower and
A lion faced her on the moonlit wall
Who roared and reached and caught and held her there.

SONG

You don't listen to what I say.
When I lean towards you in the car
You simply smile and turn away.

It's been like this most of the day,
Sitting and sipping, bar after bar:
You don't listen to what I say.

You squeeze a lemon from a tray,
And if you guess how dear you are
You simply smile and turn away.

Beyond the hairline of the bay
The steamers call that shore is far.
You don't listen to what I say:

Surely there's another way?
The waiter brings a small guitar.
You simply smile and turn away.

Sometimes I think you are too gay,
Smiling and smiling, hour after hour.
You don't listen to what I say.
You simply smile and turn away.

ALEX'S GAME

He sets the table with sponge firs in tubs –
Lung sculpture trees – and turkeys' iron fans,
A palace-garage-castle, fleets of vans
In stalls flecked yellow-red, indian clubs
Mountains, and so on. When a lorry's hubs
Swerve and blurt off their small black tyres, a lead
Farm girl with plasticine and matchstick head
Oil into midget axles smartly rubs
And fits the baby quoits again. He reaches
For a squat cowboy in red plastic breeches
Stretched round a missing horse, sets him to guard
The girl. But look what she does: up she swings
Her one stiff arm and belts the cowboy hard.
Now that wăs not in his imaginings.

ALEX AT THE BARBER'S

He is having his hair cut. Towels are tucked
About his chin, his mop scalped jokingly.
The face in the mirror is his own face.

The barber moves and chats among the green
And methylated violet, snipper-snips,
Puts scissors down, plugs in a plaited flex,

And like a surgeon with his perfumed hands
Presses the waiting skull and shapes the base.
He likes having his hair cut, and the man

Likes cutting it. The radio drones on.
The eyes in the mirror are his own eyes.
While the next chair receives the Demon Blade,

A dog-leg razor nicks a sideburn here;
As from a sofa there a sheet is whisked
And silver pocketed. The doorbell pings.

The barber, frowning, grips the ragged fringe
And slowly cuts. Upon the speckled sheet
The bits fall down and now his hair is cut.

The neighing trams outside splash through the rain.
The barber tests the spray for heat and rubs
Lemon shampoo into his spiky hair.

Bent with his head above the running bowl,
Eyes squeezed shut, he does not see the water
Gurgle and sway like twisted sweetpaper

Above the waste, but, for a moment, tows
A sleigh of polished silver parrots through
Acres of snow, exclaiming soundlessly.

Then towel round the head. Head swung gently up.
Eyes padded. As the barber briskly rubs,
The smile in the mirror is his own smile.

SNAPSHOT

A girl is twirling a parasol.
A dog is worrying a doll.

Postcards and lace shawls
Are sold by garden waterfalls.

Chopin spins from wax and horn.
The terrier bounds across the lawn,

Aching for rivers, while the doll
Gets prodded by the parasol.

Roger, fresh from soap and razor,
Approaches in his candy blazer

And strokes his Maupassant moustache:
'This July sun is really *harsh*!'

Soft and quiet as a panda,
She follows him to the verandah

Where the cool pebble lemonade
Burns and burns in a green shade.

Upon a chair of mother-of-pearl
He pulls his smiling panda girl

Into the crook of his striped arm,
His thumb upon her closing palm.

The girl puts down her parasol.
The dog swallows the doll.

GIRL WITH COFFEE TRAY

Slipping, she fell into the sitting-room,
For one gay second noticed what was there:
The salmon cushion on the lashed cane chair;
The frail greenness of apples in a gloom
Of chalk wall; round her head the watery boom
Of stool logs, crags and waves of hessian sea
Where driftwood pencils and books floated. She
Considered vaguely that the arching plume
Of her white cat's tail, too, was oceanic.
The sofa creaked. Cups smashed to smithereens.
The cat mewed like a gull, bounced off in panic.
Her feet still sprawling on the hall's wax tiles,
She cried. The seabed carpet stretched for miles
Where she lay drowning in the blues and greens.

OWLS

The murderous owls off Malo bay
Can lure a sleepless watchman to the sea,
For their deep singing may be heard
Throughout a night of thunder and their red
Eyes take him dancing silently
Down to the choking sea-bed. Far away
His heavy wife sleeps like the dead
Upon the feathers of a bird.

WAITING FOR A WIND

Save us, we cannot see. Our eyes fail us,
But through the wrong end of a telescope,
Curled up in heat with salty hair and brows

The ragged mermaids perch on sloping rocks
Beside the waves' black glitter. The sun is white
And sheets of dazzling air hang all about

Their island, tightening and thick as steam,
Scorching and bright beneath descending sky.
A mermaid dives with arms held at her side

Down to wet depths of green and sunken blue,
To spiky fish, fabulous as explosions.
Can we imagine this, not hope for vision?

Slowly, with small and round exclaiming mouth,
She bursts up glistening from the broken sea.
Colour is the liquor of her eyes.

The scene grows taller in their sweet wet flood
Of swirls and washes. Light clears with bangs.
Yes, our hands shake. Our dream boat rocks.

Her sodden globes focus the dancing air,
Pinpoint to blackness, a tiny inky dot
Held for a second till it boils and splashes

Outwards into forms of hues and flames.
Waves gulp ultramarine on mustard rocks
Trailing a lemon lichen, while sea-flowers,

(Pale lipstick colours on deep brown or sage),
Cluster in sucking clefts of rock or drift
In fronds from humps of dead-eye mussels.

Some weed is khaki-ribbon, trailing arms
Water-plunged rouge-veined with cooler blue,
Finger-nails pinched crab flakes, sticky hair

Of mermaids bleached like straw, the dryer strands
Whiter, whiter, dry as an empty ship.
The light burns. Only the sea can restore.

The world was formed within a mermaid's eyes.

THE COOK'S LESSON

When the King at last could not manage an erection,
The tables were wiped down and a banquet prepared.
The Cook was a renegade, a master of innuendo,
And was later hanged for some imaginary subversion,
Found laughing in the quarter of the filthy poor.
This, had we known it, was to be his last banquet,
And as such was fittingly dissident and experimental.
Often he had confided to us the tenets of his craft,
How a true artist is obsessed with the nature of his material,
And must make evident the process of creation in preference
To the predictable appearance of the finished product.
The charcoal-burners were lit, the porcelain laid
And the simple broths prepared in which the meal was enacted,
For this was a living meal, a biological history of food.
I cannot remember much. We sweated and fainted and were
    revived
With fragrant towels. We ate furiously and were rewarded
With knowledge of a kind we did not even recognise.
Spawn in the luke gruel divided, gilled and finned,
Swam down flowered channels to the brink of oil
And fell to the plate. Before our eyes
The litter spurted into the fire, picked out by tongs,
Eggs hatched into the soup, embryos bled,
Seeds sprouted in the spoon. As I said, we ate fast,
Far back into life, eating fast into life.
Now I understand that food is never really dead:
Frilled and forked, towered, dusted, sliced,
In mimic aspic or dispersed in sauces,
Food is something that will not willingly lie down.
The bland liquids slid over our tongues as
Heartbeats under crusts, mouthfuls of feathers.

MR AND MRS BONES

He thinks of ogre-statured Mrs Bones,
Watercolour lips, and hair in braided phones,
Chopping about with her dangerous hands,
Loading a tray with matutinal viands:
Delicate and wafer-slivered breakfast courses,
Toasted kidneys like new pigskin purses,
Folded ham, and chops with various sauces
Served with mushrumps black as hearses.
Meat sickness, it is the sickness of Greed
Who full to bursting still wants to feed,
Eating and eating with extraordinary vigour,
As though to become different we must get bigger.
O Mr Bones, growing in bed
With a pillow propped by your tea-cosy head,
Here at half-past-eight o'clock you lie
Wrapped in your breakfast like divinity.
Your knife flashes. The eiderdown groans.
O carneous Mrs, O ravenous Mr Bones.

AN EXCHANGE BETWEEN THE FINGERS
AND THE TOES

Fingers:

Cramped, you are hardly anything but fidgets.
We, active, differentiate the digits:
Whilst you are merely *little toe* and *big*
(Or, in the nursery, some futile pig)
Through vital use as pincers there has come
Distinction of the *finger* and the *thumb*;
Lacking a knuckle you have sadly missed
Our meaningful translation to a *fist*;
And only by the curling of that joint
Could the firm *index* come to have a point.
You cannot punch or demonstrate or hold
And therefore cannot write or pluck or mould:
Indeed, it seems deficiency in art
Alone would prove you the inferior part.

Toes:

Not so, my friends. Our clumsy innocence
And your deft sin is the main difference
Between the body's near extremities.
Please do not think that we intend to please:
Shut in the dark, we once were free like you.
Though you enslaved us, are you not slaves, too?
Our early balance caused your later guilt,
Erect, of finding out how we were built.
Your murders and discoveries compile
A history of the crime of being agile,
And we it is who save you when you fight
Against the odds: you cannot take to flight.
Despite your fabrications and your cunning,
The deepest instinct is expressed in running.

GREEN FINGERS

1

Last year's sticks are holding out
For more. Away with them.

The soil aches, tilting over,
Worms waving from windows.

Then seeds: fine as gunpowder,
Horny as toe-nails. A palaver.

You could say that these shoots
Have done it before: frauds.

But at five my daughter is called
To bed. I am not exactly myself.

The garden is creased with buds.
The scent inhabits the glass.

Hands are finished with the
Amazing things they recognise.

2

The pond is hideous, a mug of teeth.
Snouts and flex of lilies rot.

Mud moves with halfpenny frogs
The colour of aniseed.

We tilt the buckets out
To catch the snot of newts

And barrows heave the life away
So that the children will not drown.

Man shudders from ungovernable nature,
His greatest deceit.

After a night of unsettled dreams,
The mirror merciless in horror:

Nose. Vulnerable eyes. Growth
Of hair. The whole stirring.

HEDGE TUTOR

Consulting the calendar of hedges
Banked up higher than your head,
We seem to share the surprise of walking
On a riverbed.

Our hands touch the flowers, shocked:
A clutch of folded fern, a brief
Violet, crumpled like a girl's
Handkerchief.

And we lean to ourselves, and to
These rituals that love condemns
Us to, gathering until the hand
Is hot with stems.

Somewhere a long way back it began.
It spun and clustered, divided and broke.
The woods made way, your eyes softened
And the hedges spoke:

'We do not suffer. Roots are lodged.
We prophesy the past and free
The future from its curious bond
As history.

This is what we are and were.
You, like us, powerless to change,
Walk in the given garden. The rest
Time will arrange.'

Thick light and wet, a gradient's pull
Past the invisible coughing cows,
Shoes plastered with grass,
Back to the house:

Shall we be ashamed? You are scared
By the gassed turnip heads beneath a stile,
Take my arm tighter, hurry through the rain
With a homeward smile

To the timed clock and the caged flower,
The raincoats hung, the table laid;
The different books half-lit beneath
A single shade.

No one believes more than a tiny tract.
In the delirium of silence the vast extenses
Wheel inwards to you, the presumable
Spiral's axis.

MANZU

A girl is seated, nude and placid, lost
In quietness. The pig-tail thick and full
On flashlit shoulder-blades. The ankles crossed.
Lifesize, exact, supremely animal.

This lean and virginal formality,
A poised ragazza on a rush-seat chair,
Finds cloistral echoes. From a trinket tree
Chickens and saints puncture the thumbed-out air

And dolphins on the slow cathedral doors
Plunge like a drowning scalp. Within their globe,
Bemitred dancers tip-toe and then pause.
The cardinal is sensual in his robe:

One sees beneath embroidery bare toes
As long as fingers. Youthful age imparts
That faintly turnip shadow to his nose,
That silent smile, affinity of parts.

The buds are breaking. No one is annoyed.
It is a simple drama. Lavish, yes,
But white and delicate. And eyes avoid
The bland Italian ritual of flesh.

OBJET TROUVÉ: PIAZZA SAN MARCO

We've seen St Mark's personal foot
Encased within a silver boot:
A window gave on to the bone
Just like an operation
Performed with grace for jewelled feet,
And though it did not seem complete
(The boot abrupt, the relic brittle)
The object made the most of little
And challenged our aesthetic sense
With a luxurious reticence.
So we imagined that it told
With gruesome tact how in the old
Days God removed his Saints with haste
From the slow martyrdoms they faced,
How Mark rose upwards through the air
Out of his feet left standing there,
How round his pretty feet they built this square.

REVOLUTION

Celestial jig and orphic toot:
Elizabethans meant to please.
The vocal round and fingered lute
Reflected godly harmonies.

When oratorios of brass
Later erupted with the plague,
Like the expansive Middle Class
Their provenance seemed bright and vague.

But music of the baroque type
Evolved from cruel instruments:
The hangman's drum, the bosun's pipe,
The horn, – curled for convenience.

Thus purged into its trilling were
Emotions of the rope and chase,
As wigs replaced the natural hair
And formalised each pitted face.

Lost was the music of the spheres:
The heavens now extended far
Beyond these little human fears,
Beyond the frantic orchestra.

PRIMARY SOURCE

The Duchess complains her children die too young,
A pastoral counterpoint to infant labour.
The Tutor sympathises, holds his tongue,
Himself an offspring of the factory neighbour.
Blood wrestles with blood, and class with class.
Those threads of black against the hill's green throat
Which prompted her conceit, like a forged note
Damage his useful innocence. They pass
The mortgaged oaks of the old Duke's estate.
'Youth is ambitious,' she exclaims, 'age vile,
Dependent. Do not confuse my amorous fate
With history!' The Duchess turns to smile
And rests her chin, half-stern, upon his shoulder,
As if to stop him growing any older.

LANDSCAPES OF WESTERN NEW YORK

1 *Lake Chautauqua*

Behind the sheeted lake the deer
Pose, whose forests pencilled-in
Contain quiet ambuscades of snow,
The tracks and berries they defend.

Skiers drop above the town
Where bubble elevators rise
And demerara tyre-treads squeeze
Their perfect diamonds, parked for lunch.

The hotel clinks its empty beer
And clocks eject the curls and slacks
To buckle juddering steel and crouch
At speed by telescoping barns.

Night sees the hotel desolated.
Smoking at a corner table
The waiters eat what no one ordered:
Soft cheese, expensive quarto steaks.

While from sedans a mile away
The skiers serenade the deer,
And in the dark the hard white lake
Stands still among delighted trees.

2 *Niagara Falls*

Fierce aquatic carelessness!
Your great arenas celebrate
The sensible decision of river
To undergo a sudden fate.

What struggle there has been is done.
The rapids gather for the ledge.
From ragged foam and rocks we see
How huge the force, how bulked the edge,

How ropes of crystal braided over
Quiver, continuously thick,
Spilling to thinness in the depth,
A change as skilful as a trick.

The conjuring light falls through the spray
And ghosts of equilibrists quail.
The graded colours curve down where
Imaginary barrels sail.

We look and gasp, and are deceived.
This stagey routine fails at length
To signify what it had meant:
The waters' wilful, sickening strength.

3 *Buffalo*

The metered tarmac elevates
Its clean technologies, distils
The whiff of chemicals, a mile
Of steel. And Erie shrugs the stains.

Far from the shore a city collapses
Into its suburbs: four-garage
Colonial, and shops for tartan.
Executives flop into pools.

Industry and avenue:
The civic idea pacifies
The furies. Winking boulevards
Offer a dangerous escape.

For tourists, curios and wreckers
Assert a kind of grammar, cars
Smooth past hotels coloured as cake,
A wilderness of lowered shades.

Warmed by the sobbing of the lights
We reach the core, a cut-price noon,
The taste of our solicitude,
The negro store, the golden dome.

4 *Letchworth Park*

Car horns on the scenic whorls
Puncture the coloured woods. Behind,
A weeping smoke of water spills
Through photographic crevices.

A vegetable empire drifts
Against pathetic monuments
To local rape and torturing.
The air is warm and fine with rain.

Like someone else's shoes the strange
Utensils of the pioneers:
The women come in Steinberg hats
To view the maps and dusty churns

And creep with ten-cent postcards on
The car park's sodden botany
While unfamiliar feral sounds
Disturb the undergrowth beyond.

The land is governed. The rain falls.
This love of history preserves
The sewn eyes of the Indian,
Fearless in their bright false glass!

IN KENTUCKY

White wooden paling, the tremolo organ:
Marlins and family glassily stare
From the panelled walls of a Kentucky room
Furiously shuttered against the glare.

Beneath the racing Dufy clouds
A portico invokes the past.
Daughter and children visit the mansion.
Bourbon settles in a silver glass.

We love you, we love you still, Miss Lucy,
The phantoms of the house declare.
Though pretty farms turn real estate
And you have grown, we need you where

Plucked acres measured to the post
Extend beyond your hammock's lull
And horses' names like battleships'
Fade red upon the barn's flaked hull.

Though there is shouting in the lane
The painted summer is not dead,
For look! your iron negro grins,
The jockey cap upon his head!

PICTURES FROM A '48 DE SOTO

1

Humped in this swart sedan, paper half-lowered,
The automatic at my side snug as a cancer,
I watch the house. Or in the house myself

Look at my wrist, insane with jealousy:
Her furs and veils lie on the front seat,
The tongue inside its curious second home.

Even banked high in snow, the engine dead,
The woven greenish braids and tassels swing.
A razored head lurches, lolls back, headlights

Shattered in the pursued and silent mirror.
The windows are shut: palms thud wildly on
The glass. Black opening mouth, the sound switched off.

2

The last owner lugged gravel, the wings
Rusted and bolted back. We drive it
Three thousand miles to the Pacific

Where the blind nude hulk, down to its canvas,
Like a slow fist hisses into the dump.
Now the yellow plates illegally decorate

The bathroom, and these, too, fetch improbable ghosts:
After days on the anvil, tanking through the dust,
We arrive at the coloured river. Our eyes hurt.

Dwarfs wrestle behind glass. Dresses
Are cut to the buttocks' cleft. Half-shaved men
Are running sheeted through the empty square.

FLOOD BOX

Wheels grind on the shingle. Round
And round the drenched machinery
Propels its oily bulk. The sound
Screams. The train enters the sea.
Blanched fingers from the bath, cold teeth
In softened gums and floating hair:
Down the Landscape of Underneath
The paradigms of panic stare.

Imagined depth! Within its grip
White figures struggle to be free.
Above, the motorboats unzip
Their tinted wrinkled scenery
And breakers fall like piano lids,
Unloosing liquid horrors: black
Regency-hair crabs, snotty squids
And cherub penises of wrack.

Or think of water running clear
Over moss channel, dyke and bed;
The torches lit along the pier,
A liquid garden, pale and red:
The tempo slows, a pulse pretends
To measure out eternity
But no formality extends
The haggard ebbing of the sea.

Cones of the city, smoke and rain.
A net of amber rivers breaks
The water into shapes, but pain
Is built against the narrowing lakes:
The fevered cemetery bell
Mocks at the surface of the deep.
The leaping shadows sharply smell,
Terraqueous shadows of your sleep.

You turn upon your matchbox bed,
Your knees against the door, the lamp
A glare of violence at your head.
The walls bend outward with the damp.

Some flood inlays the solid floor
And chairs achieve the sense of stilts.
The slow meniscus at the door
Soon shoulders rats and sodden quilts!

Too soon, too soon, and yet you choose
To break the skin, and once the skin
Is broken nothing's left to lose.
You shiver in a dream of fin,
The blood leaked out, the mirrors free
Of your still figure, grinning, torn:
While you enact a scenery
Of silent quanting down the lawn.

You need a pause to recollect,
But speed denies what's lost amid
A sobbing urgency now checked
By closing inches of the lid.
The lungs are stretching to be free,
Down past the dimly burning light.
Open the window to the sea,
Push from the ceiling to the night!

Hands fluttering, you fade away
With an imaginary flute
Like a wood ghost, and what you say
Is lost among the final hoot
As you explode the busy robe
Of bones. Ours is a futile chase:
The limits of your endless globe
Magnify the dismal face.

Turn to the back. No one is right.
The dream contains us from the start.
The brain rehearses out of sight
The tender habit of the heart.
The room remains, embalmed and still
Like a sunk ship, and what we find
Impossible is the firm will
In the drowned shape you leave behind.

THE PIT

From the beginning, the egg cradled in pebbles,
The drive thick with fledglings, to the known last
Riot of the senses, is only a short pass.
Earth to be forked over is more patient,
Bird hungers more, flower dies sooner.

But if not grasped grows quickly, silently.
We are restless, not remembering much.
The pain is slow, original as laughter,
Reaching for all of it, hardly aware,
Beginning again and feeling for its terrain.

We were often told and still we would not listen,
And closing fingers, those accomplices,
Took comfort from a lie. From lap to grass
Whining, motionless on the lowest branch
Above the pine needles, climbing the heather:

We did not listen. It hid there still to find.
Much since was hard to get, later displeased,
Nursing an ordinary complaint or waiting
For a reiterated brilliance,
Growing in ignorance, too near to see.

Now in the suburbs windows are on fire,
Pale globes quiver on their dusty strings
And afternoons disperse with mirth of gnome,
The rigid stabbed flamingo pink in the trees,
Split to the touch and walking by the pool.

Now life jerking in its sustained coda
Constricts its furniture and its events.
The frowning bus disappears down the hill
Or slides before the window with its bored
Passengers staring unashamedly in.

Now above the trees the ice-cream's bare
Electric tongue stammers its recitation.
Children run out in the dumb-bell cul-de-sac
To their cold delight, skipping between the turds
Of long-dead dogs, coiled thickly on the stone.

The children learn so quickly. The house stirs.
Swallows leave earlier, apples to be pressed.
Half the sky burns: the other half is dark.
Hair pushing slowly out, generations
Surrounding us with wonder, theirs and ours.

Nothing to give, nothing has been learnt.
The past simply denies the urge for a truce,
Creeping into the egg. When it is time
We can appoint a committee for the feasts,
And for the next year's feasts, and the year after.

Locks stick, glass metamorphosed
In leafy caryatids of summer where
Heat packs the panes and fingers tremble in
Tobacco pockets, a tomato sniffed,
Its greenish acid bloom and tiny hairs.

The pain stirs again like a new life
To be unravelled. It had to come to this.
The body is nothing, the body thinks nothing,
The short senses grubbing on their sticks
Feel nothing, the forgotten carioca.

A line moves to the finger end, and curls,
Head fallen in helplessness. The wails
Of children break behind the woven fences,
Those minted faces far beyond our sight.
The gates shut: a parade of Japanese flags.

And alive on the porch the councillor lowers his pipe,
Comes down from the dunes a bathroom Arab
Firing off caps, or crouched over shells
Gathered in sodden pumps, the soprano waitress
Bringing hot tea across the evening sand.

The nights come in slowly. Behind a half-curtain
The impossible is completed. A single lamp
Weighs down its ornaments in pools of light.
Shadows crawl over the crater, roped
To the terrain's recoil, roped to the pit.

THE TWO SISTERS

He saw her fingers in the candlelight
Crooked with the needle, poised to break a thread,
Or at her temple pressed to ease the sight,
With one thin strand of hair loose from her head
Falling in its tiredness, cedar red,
Across the bent and pale half-humorous face,
Hair like a precious garment of the dead
Tucked now behind the ear into its place,
An automatic gesture yet with grace
To make a ceremony of her task
When fingers smoothing down the finished lace
Are answered by the question that they ask
Of labour's quiet satisfaction, such
As simply sanctifies the sight and touch.

That one he loved, the other in a dream
Possessed his spirit, though she never smiled;
One with rolled sleeves or lost in linen's steam,
Fruit in her apron for the orphaned child,
The other walking by herself, beguiled
By passing beggars and by horoscopes;
That home to him, this every day more wild;
One was his shelter, one played out his hopes,
A mind that grasps uncertainty and gropes
For wind-wide vistas from delirious rocks
While others go no further than the slopes
On which they tend the necessary flocks.
Both sisters were his world. From each he learned
What man must die from. And to both returned.

Her sister wasn't helpful, that was certain,
Lying with headaches on her bed all day,
The neighbours wondering at the fastened curtain,
At the strange girl who only knelt to pray
With steps to scrub and the day's fires to lay,
Who stared at breakfast, had no time to spend
In gutting fish and could not see her way
To lay the table for her brother's friend.

The world would take more than one life to mend,
The other thought: there simply wasn't time
To moon about the inevitable end,
For death remained as private as a crime
And as improbable, so long as life
Whitened her knuckles that enclosed the knife.

They told her not think about the fish.
The fish was simply something they could eat.
It had to die to turn into a dish.
Once dead there was no memory in meat.
She bit her lip, muttered and left her seat,
Her plate untouched. Apologies were made,
A mention of her efforts and the heat:
No wonder nerves were just a little frayed.
But who foresaw as she did death's curved blade
Casting its shadow on the company
And their autumnal guest whose hands displayed
The future's frightening leap, his ruined tree?
Her brother lost to him, white as a sheet,
Her sister still, devoted, at his feet.

And now as if a promise were fulfilled,
Insistently, uncruel, even with joy,
As children tread the towers that they build
And love the crouching cat that they annoy,
Death with his conjuror's fingers took the boy
And left his body still, as one might leave
Forgotten in its box a broken toy.
Mourning has very little to achieve:
A neighbour wiped his eye upon his sleeve
And friends came to console them for their loss.
The sisters found that they could better grieve
If death were seen as swaddling pinned across
His face. They moved their fingers to the brooch
That held it there. Their hope was a reproach.

Death was the knowledge that eluded him,
The senses stunned to feel the body cease,
The spirit sobbing in the missing limb,
The sisters exiled from their brother's lease

And its reversion. In the perfumed peace
Of living's shadow nothing was revealed.
He realized the strangeness would increase
As time unwound its laps about the field
Where he pursued again the power that healed
Its stubborn strokes: those hands laid on his death
Were lent themselves to death and so unsealed
At once his own and every stifled breath
To speak, amazed, of what life was about.
And turned the everlasting inside out.

He was still alive. And the sisters passed
Silently and with great joy into
The landscape of his unbound eyes at last.
One in the wisdom of her insight knew
How life describes its need to be thought true
In terms of its illusions, and she made
Her happiness the air to which she grew.
The other was content to live in shade,
Grew downwards, desperately, undisplayed.
Both were his nature. That he understood.
Perhaps uncertain, even half-afraid
Which to embrace, he knew that both were good,
As on his heel, beneath his wrinkled skull,
Moved the creased sweating happy miracle.

So when the perfume filled the house she smiled
Inside herself. It was the good part. Both
Were good. She was excited as a child
Though busy with preparing food and loath
To leave it. Someone present swore an oath
It would have paid a labourer for a year,
But who could measure growing against growth,
Or time the seed against the waving ear?
And now one knew it, what was death to fear
But this extraordinary ritual where
Its moment was acknowledged to be near,
Its mystery by a sister's healing hair
Divulged? To smile was to betray her sense
Of love in perfume, tears, experience.

LECTURE ROOM: TEN AM

Robed in black, like surgeons already in mourning
For a dramatic failure in our usual techniques,
Amputation of Wordsworth or extraction of impacted Keats,
We hold precious as the last candle carried in cupped hand
The notion that here, at this place and at this time,

The twin tyrants of passage and location with their goads,
The murderous rubato, the spiritual ampallang,
Might for once be cheated of their inevitable victory
And something simple and other, like a flickering flame,
Be held a moment for surprised contemplation.

They are not appeased. Their anchors weigh down hands and
    eyes
To abject homage before their disgusting achievements.
Amusement, idleness, study: all are irrelevant
Since the black conspiracy equally absorbs them all,
And the life that should be shocked and free is still tame.

The heroes are shown not to falter, or to falter superbly,
And voices from all the rooms rise gradually through the walls
In acknowledgment of the cult which binds us:
' 'Tis not contrary to reason to prefer the destruction
Of the whole world to the scratching of my finger.'

'The last passage is not yet sufficiently explicated.'
'No one has ever seen the female palingenia:
Fecundated before even getting rid of her nymph's corset,
She dies with her eyes still shut,
At once mother and infant, in swaddling clothes.'

EXAMINATION ROOM: TWO PM

All the ingredients of interrogation, green baize,
Papers strewn with care, faces averted in unconcern,
Impossible questions: these establish and then relax
The identity-conditions. Thus, as colours are real
When we say 'red' and 'yellow', and yet are hard to find

Within such generalities, so the predication of interrogation
Locates the candidate only within those classes of candidate
To which he may with safety be admitted, and today
All the submissive accidentals, fainting, beauty, garrulity
And wrong clothes, are simply the material for anecdotes.

The old hate the young for believing them to be really old.
The young hate the old for knowing that they are in fact young.
Both are dangerously polite. Only these must for the moment
    suffer:
All aggression, all curiosity, all friendship is put aside.
They weep with gratitude, with laughter and with being hurt.

UPPER READING ROOM: SIX PM

In the guilty half-silence of this long
Waiting-room, allusions buzz for us
Like flies, chairs scrape back for topics leaving
From a different platform. Lugging each hero's baggage,
We lie: 'I am like you. You are alive in me.'

Kipper-tied quinquagenarians, tramps
With satchels, academic teeny-boppers
Their carrels piled with hats and avocados,
Knee-locked civil servants of apparatus,
Nuns: we are shades that have lasted one more day.

And our eyes meet over the low partitions
In tentative love, sharing our furtive sense
Of the insults of that antagonist with whom
We ever contrive grandmaster draws, who sets
The problems that we compromise, from whom

We all on some long morning learned the rules.
He stains the stones. The scaffold streams with him.
Leggy girls on their venerable monosyllables
Are led by him to a gagging dryness. Boys
Smooth their balding heads, invoking his praises.

He brings the wrinkled clean expatriates
To the dug-outs of a mad ambition, shading
Their narrowed eyes on the beaches of exegesis,
Saying: 'We will return.' He likes to see
A gulping of tesseracts and Gondals in

Our crazed search across sands of the impossible
For the undying, and he annotates
Pistacia terebinthus to a sacrament,
Its sweet stench long evaporated
In the pages of a demythologized

Indexed kerygma. But we refuse to be bullied,
Even as hammers slog the walls crumbling
Around us. Books are about life, and life
Is somewhere here. On paper. In eyes. Somewhere.
So now we stack our cards. We reserve our defence.

THE CHOIR MASTER

Alkman, Seventh Century BC

Oh my sweet girls, dear girls, with your so clear round voices
Linked in the sounds I taught you, your eyes on the page
And all the air no Siren struck with such compulsion
Alive in my ear like the breath of our own Kalliope
Without whose favour dance is graceless, no song moving,
Whose name is always on my lips, and is your name
My dears, as I urge you on like horses to your goal.

Now my legs fail me, standing in the colonnade
Clutching my black heart. If only I could be a bird!
An unharmed gazed-at bird, the colour of distant water,
A bird not alone but flying in easy neighbourhood,
A noble cormorant or tilted migrant gull,
Each far wave bursting for a moment into flower,
Oh my singing pupils, flowers of the sea's same song!

I am old. Your hands slip into mine for friendship
And you sing of the new life, all that I cannot teach.
For there are three seasons: summer and winter, and autumn is
      three,
But in the new life when buds come there is no satisfaction,
Fruit and harvest, none, and no store. Spring is an ache,
In spring the mountains break down and weep, the snowdrop
Turns away, heavy with grief. And I clutch my heart,

My heart which is like spring lightning in the mountains when
A lantern is dashed to the ground and the gods roar with
      laughter.
In my dream I am rooted and a witness, amazed and curious:
They bring a simple dairy churn, though cast in gold,
And you, my dears, fill it yourselves with the milk of a lioness!
And proceed to turn out a monstrous cheese which Hermes
      himself
Might well have had appetite for after he'd murdered Argos!

Ah well, my own tastes are simple enough. Something like
      porridge
Suits me now. You I've groomed and coaxed, my dear sisters,
It's no wonder your skills and beauty astound me still,

As hooves, as wings. You think me an old owl chunnering
In an attic, perhaps, or dare I hope as a ship's pilot
As we steer with one voice like a swan on the streams of
   Xanthus,
Oh my dear girls, Kallope's daughters, my daughters, my music.

SCENARIO FOR A WALK-ON PART

The borrowed walking-stick that makes me lame,
The single curiously worn-down tyre,
The hanging button and forgotten name,
The grinning of the vulnerable liar:
These are the gambits of a chosen game,
A well-cut personality on hire,
Mirrors too low, the eyebrows graze the frame,
Warming my hands before an unlit fire.

Dinner a skirmish, legs uncrossed and crossed,
An alp of linen and the sight of nylons,
Pudding arriving full of fruit and frost,
And, swimming in their syrup, smoking islands,
Lips at a silver spoon proclaim me lost,
My single joke counters a threat of violence.
The table cleared, I cannot count the cost
Of dinner or of nerves. The rest is silence.

Now in the sharpest lock at close of day,
Hands as if manacled, the gravel spurting,
My hosts with linked arms waving me away,
The gulf of what I didn't say still hurting
(Since you are only known by what you say),
Yawning beneath my silent murmur skirting
The dangerous excuse, the wish to stay,
Like the evasions of protracted flirting:

Alone I drive away with my awareness
That once again I've failed the magic word
Whose demon locks me up inside my bareness,
The charming openness unsaid, unheard.
Is love the better for its hurts and rareness?
I frown and think so. Falling into third
On a hill, I glimpse a face: the sheer unfairness
Fights with my sense of shame at being stirred.

The sexy minister reclaims his scarf,
A girl in denim runs to meet a train,
Mrs Jocasta bastes the fatted calf,
The guests have taken to their beds again:

I hold the floor but nobody will laugh,
No one is there to kiss if I complain,
I enter only in the second half,
Unwilling, underwritten, used to pain.

HER MORNING DREAMS

I trail in my sculpted sheets to the misty window
And rub a patch there like a liquid bruise.
Yes. Stooping in blue. Propped bicycle.

But absence is your only sort of news.
Over the toast and the slit boring letters
The damp end flares in ribbons like a fuse.

What do I think? Do I think it matters?
Do I think what matters? Do I think?
Oh yes, I think. Don't worry, you wouldn't notice.

The unmade bed. Finger on my pink.
Dead as he groaned upon a linen ocean,
Who would have thought he had such little ink?

Dreams for you. The head is cut in walking.
Sour puffballs. Clouds of dust.
It's a bad day for any sort of singing.

I thought that you were someone I could trust.
I can begin. Well, I can try beginning
If only somebody will say I must.

Are you my pal? Are you Ardent Ardvaark?
At first I took you for the kind who while
He sobs sinks fangs, while he sings does murder

In blue clothes, greets with insinuating smile
Across the gravel with his hands extended
In preacher or in nightclub singer style

Under a pained yet cheerful load of welcome.
Now you are someone in my morning dreams.
I was so bored that summer. Can you imagine

Life shrunk and wrinkled to its seams,
Its hopes on threads, its memories in pockets,
The sluggish mouth disowning all its streams?

Can you imagine the clean shock of naming,
And love acknowledging its paradigm?
With you misery had as little meaning

As backfriends to fingers galloping in time
With the Catalan pupil of the Neapolitan master,
Each note as true as an expected rhyme.

Perhaps you never meant that sort of magic,
Perhaps the fault was mine, grateful allure
Scoring a million in the cheated darkness,

Pretending the experience was pure.
God help us, darling, aren't we only human?
Kiss me again and let's be really sure.

I believe all disasters now, believe all pain.
As for your life, however much you hate it,
However bad it smells upon your bed,

You simply cannot go back and create it:
Something will tell you that you have to cry,
Something will tell you this was always fated.

So I have tried beginning. Or is it ending?
Things I remember cover me with shame,
They linger obstinately every morning.

Stupid. But every day it is the same.
And nothing felt like that is ever final.
Not you. Not me. Nobody is to blame.

Dreams. You walking down a dusty pavement.
Your head is always strangely turned away,
Carried as though bandaged, with little movement.

Now is the time to say it: nothing to say.
You came and went with carefully rolled forearms.
You held life in their empty space that day.

I pad from bed to stove to fill a pan.
Sometimes a step is just a step too far:
No time to think what it has got you into.

Even the job of knowing where you are
Becomes a full-time dangerous occupation.
It's honey at the bottom of the jar

But no one can be sure until it's eaten.
Not everything is right. What's possible?
I pull the whole drawer of my mind down on

My foot. Hell. The cat's beneath the bedspread
Like a blister, showing that you have gone.
I walk from room to room, trying the answer:

One from two is wrong, and one from one
Is neater. Morning dreams are calmer weeping.
All my indignities spill from the sun.

Listen to it now. All night like wedded chaos.
The creeper's down, the storm makes such a fuss.
Trying to count the blows of rain is useless.

I shall sit it out, here by the misty glass,
Till I can face the morning's empty graces,
The window sill become an abacus.

ABERPORTH

Sky is performing feats of weather over
Hills wooded to the top, humped private hills
Whose birds look down not up. Briar's between
The fields: he keeps the eating sheep from knowing
What's on the other side. Beneath the path
A culvert runs, hidden for fifty years:
Some work will dig it up again.

Yes, nature is incurious, we know.
The butterflies as big as prayerbooks draw
No lesson from the india wings they thumb through,
While chapel slate aches with its uglification
Of primrose and violet, and the gold-black graves
Make even death elaborate and absurd
Like a bad conjuror.

The sea is much visited here, whose colours are cooler
And life uncertain as well it might be in
The earth's tears. Gulls on the sand look sharp.
Without anxiety the jellyfish is hideously still,
And the same could be said of the cliffs where wind carries
The loves of freewheeling crickets across a haze
Of sun-baked blackberries.

But we so easy are still not at our ease:
Such closeness open to us as though to a
Laconic Christ, hands flat to the ears with pity!
How we wish not to judge, wish for the starlight
And its emblems, the foliage globose and witchy,
With sounds coming nearer (Frrr! Frrr!) speaking
Of something that might content us.

GHOST VILLAGE

Something takes me away, even from the spotlit
Indian clubs of our small happy government,
The gasp of hope and memory's applause,
In brown rooms, in yellow rooms, in red rooms by the sea,
To the colourless and soundless world we half-remember.

Presaged and annotated by our paltry sobs,
Older than all the lives we know or ever knew,
So sharply critical of the success of matter,
Keeping its own activities a deadly secret,
It is blind and alert as the black eyes of negatives.

Something said somewhere at some time is not enough
To appease its absorbing interest in what we did not mean
To old friends suddenly noticed as they glance up from books
With the sort of look which asks nothing because it is not worth
    it,
By the curled sea in rooms we shall half-forget.

Old friends in new rooms, new friends in old rooms:
It sees them come and go, because it is not worth it,
But a path down the valley cracked with grass
Brings us to the ghosts who must be faced,
Who questioned the blind world and would not let it lie.

Ghosts have hunters, but the hunters lose the track,
For the craned neck does not suspect a reply
And the star or the heron is never asked if it requires
To be looked at, by those who glance up from books
When the curtains are drawn back from the evening sky.

Friendless, rootless by choice, they made a home for this bay
Where pairs of stone windows were set to frown at the sea
With all the gloomy unconcern of self-absorbed exiles
Whose delineation of the jealousies and dribbled ghylls
Only betrayed their real longing and peculiar laughter.

Did neighbours wonder at the striding, the leaping of gates?
Did Squire Tribute, coming from beyond the ridge
Where the harnessed pismire superb in its plumes of dust
Pretended to be a horse on a careless errand,
Judge? Or was it changed, the outside world?

When Mistress Tidings courted Sinful the Silent
And whispers sent sidling three sides of the square
Returned across the gap, shocked and delighted,
Was it too much like what had always been known
To make much sense, the inside world?

For we have known that difference as well,
Hands drumming impatiently on green baize
As we listen to the next to last report,
The tank brimming, the wipers running freely,
Set for the coast and the foul pinks of love.

They took the mountain for its broken counterpart.
Steamers visited the creaking pier and the washed gravel
Lay heaped like wheat on the shore of their closed lives.
In front rooms hands were folded on knees. A ticking clock
Enlarged the stone silences, defining a central gravity.

They saw the cow turn her tail into a handle,
Replenishing three or four fields beside a cliff,
And resolved as they walked alone at evening in watchchains
To make their lives acceptable to others, their deaths
Only to themselves. And the fields steamed with joy.

Their children were the first to make shy advances,
Wove with fingers, were pinioned, wept, touched,
Cruelly accused the unhappy of being only unhappy,
Talked incessantly of the marriage of headland and valley
And thought of nothing much to say, but learned to read.

Until one day these became themselves the brooding exiles,
The best cap square set or the downed pick at noon,
The mountain unshaped with interjections of dynamite,
Tired of responsibility, dreaming, easily wounded,
Crying out to be, and being, successfully lured by cities.

Nothing is changed, and most of the dancing is still glum
In neighbouring villages where they watch and wait
For the silver band to assemble in the Sunday dusk.
Nothing is changed, when wishes are fulfilled
And again we stare into the boiling centre.

Nothing is changed, but everything will alter
And the blind world exults as we expect it should
Over the first and last, the inside and the outside,
The forms and secrets, friends and generations,
Pacts made by ghosts that some of us have tried to love.

So thinking, a tiny swivelling figure in the bay,
Hands in pockets, turning over stones with a holiday foot,
Posed between the unravelling tides and the abandoned houses,
Made an uncertain gesture, ceased watching the sea,
And plodded up the hill for company.

TO ANGUS MACINTYRE

From windy *Llanaelhaiarn* to
Far *Achaglachgach* just a few
Nocturnal stanzas penned for you.
      The form is Scottish
And pocket-sized to suit those who
      Live in a cottage.

Achaglachgach – is that right?
Too many achs? Too few? You might
Get headed paper. In this light
      I'm going blind
Wondering how many achs to write.
      Ach, never mind.

As dons grow stout from small successes
Put out by academic presses
To catch the textbook boom, my guess is
      They'll all buy places
With unpronounceable addresses
      In open spaces.

By disused pits, on bogs and moors,
Are shacks for sale with earthen floors.
It hardly matters that the doors
      Are off their hinges
As long as they're within, of course,
      The Celtic fringes.

Nature is all around and *so* near,
For us from *Brecon* to *Snowdonia*,
For you from *Skye* to *Caledonia*.
      We often go,
And the exertion makes us bonier,
      Nicer to know.

Although the landscape's much enjoyed,
Still a few fields are unemployed:
Campers are not now much annoyed
      By concrete Gents
And where there isn't one, avoid
      Pitching their tents.

They bring air-beds and doilies, pink
Paraffin, the kitchen sink . . .
And these are just the sort who think
    It would be deathly
To usher *Rio Tinto Zinc*
    Into *Dolgellau*.

Expecting *Wales* to be like *Borrow*
Has filled the tourist with deep sorrow
(It will be twice as bad tomorrow).
    An unspoilt view's
Unlikely as an uncleaned *Corot*,
    A falcon's news.

There once were eagles here, don't worry.
They must have left in quite a hurry.
Now only buzzards wheel and scurry
    Over *Gurn Ddu*.
Trig points on every peak? *Eryri*,
    How we mourn thee!

Are we much better? Aren't we fakers
Pacing about our fenced-off acres?
Aren't we the economic *Quakers*
    In a cold war
Between the strikers and strike-breakers?
    What are we for?

A rustic view in *Coed-y-Brenin*?
A waste to keep a cow or hen in?
What about all the jobless men in
    The National Parks?
(I make no reference to *Lenin*
    Or *Karl Marx*.)

The unemployed are twelve per cent
In *Blaenau* where the rain squalls dent
A century's slag, a broken tent
    Of splintered slate.
I wonder where the profits went,
    And who to hate.

Too late for accusations. While
Someone somewhere made a pile,
It's part of an extinct life-style.
     The simple proof?
Compare the outlay on a tile
     And a slate roof.

It's no one's quickie in the *City*,
It can't be saved by a Committee,
And yet because of this unpretty
     Straggling town
Most of *England*'s dry. Pity
     To let it drown.

I think of you in wilder greenery,
Indulging in gentlemanly venery
In miles and miles of private scenery
     With gun and rod.
You'd think old workings and machinery
     Completely odd.

How was your reading party? Tough?
Did you decide once was enough
Or will your pupils call your bluff
     And come next year?
Was it like something out of *Clough*,
     But not so queer?

Plunging clean limbs into the burn,
Steering superbly from the stern
Or watching in the reeds for tern
     While you complain
They haven't got the wits to learn
     Your line on *Paine?*

Poor dears, just now we're dipping lambs
While they in *Oxford* on their hams
Are sweating through sub-fusc exams:
     Though quite reviving,
Sabbaticals are really shams,
     A form of skiving.

A chance to swim and look less pale
Or hit the *US* lecture trail,
Modestly – from *Smith* to *Yale* –
    Or quirkily –
Risking co-eds at *Texas*, gaol!
    At *Berkeley*.

I'm glad we didn't cross the pond
For though the Dollar waves its wand
I feel somehow we've gone beyond
    That second salary,
And if of greens I'm fairly fond,
    Not greenery-yallery.

Those close-kept manuscripts we need,
Acquired through academic greed
For home-grown PhDs to read:
    Well, let them lie.
They'll wait – while *Texas* barons bleed
    Our history dry.

Sweating in seminars is not
The nicest way of being hot.
The company of one is what
    I hold most dear:
The summer's rotten, but we've got
    A hammock here.

Our estivation with our books
In our respective rural nooks
Like nearly all our actions looks
    Like compromise.
We have our alibis, like crooks
    When someone dies.

And do we like the life we chose?
Might as well ask the blowsy rose
If it approves the way it grows
    When autumn's near.
At least I don't suppose it shows
    When we're up here.

Or does it? We're as incognito
As is the *CIA* in *SEATO*,
A worker Jesuit in *Quito*
        Selling pardons
Or trilbied *Emperor Hirohito*
        In *Kew Gardens*.

With luck we can avoid being hated.
Perhaps our kind are merely fated
Smilingly to be tolerated
        Like lunatics –
Not dangerous but dissipated,
        Not keen to mix.

–Except our worlds like cocktails: loath
To give up either we live both,
One for yield and one for growth.
        *Contemptae domin-
        us splendidior rei* quoth
        The happy Roman.

Let's keep them well apart. Too late
Unwittingly you'll recreate
The one world in the other. Wait
        Until those craven
Oxford rituals infiltrate
        Your Scottish haven.

You'll be Vice-Chancellor, fit station
To rule your woolly congregation
Where you'll be welcome like an Asian
        In liberal *Kenya*
And baa'ed through your inauguration
        At *Creag*'s encaenia.

Prelims in shearing. Every lamb
Must pass. Lectures for ewe and ram
On weaving skills, plus diagram
        Of warp and weft.
At breakfast circulate the jam
        From right to left.

There will be several printed rules
On what the cows may wear in Schools,
And only three-legged milking stools
        Will be allowed.
For ignorance of farming tools,
        Fields will be ploughed.

I won't go on. It isn't true.
Nor is its opposite, where you
Take sandwiches to Hall and do
        What you are able
To climb up to a decent view
        From High Table.

Or poke your pupils with a straw
To see if they're alive, and bore
Them with all kinds of country lore
        Not known in books
And imitations of the caw
        Of various rooks.

The academic's one excuse is
He knows about the gastric juices,
Suppression of the anacrusis
        And *Ararat*.
Such subjects no doubt have their uses:
        Leave it at that.

If these impinge on *haute cuisine*,
A deathless verse or the Unseen,
If there's a soul in the machine
        To prove me wrong,
Well, that's OK, but we've both been
        Around too long.

For it's not only earth that's cooling,
Something commands us to quit fooling,
Not facts but truth we should be pooling
        In the global village
(Though I'm not one for the de-schooling
        Of *Father Illich*).

Where has the living starlight gone?
The owls are loud where once it shone.
We see the archetypal don
    Pen in his cloister
A footnote to a footnote on
    Ralph Roister Doister.

We need some vision to achieve,
A heart to wear upon our sleeve,
We need a holy spell to weave,
    Some sacred wood
Where we can teach what we believe
    Will do us good.

I see you smile. All right, it's late.
But, Angus: though it lies in wait
With terrible reproaches, fate
    May yet forgive
Our scared retreats, both small and great,
    And let us live.

UP AND DOWN

1

This is where it begins:
A cairn marks the place
Where sky negotiated
A hasty truce.

Thrown up like apophthegms
Of a phlegmatic culture
During some geological
Tedious prologue

They shoulder for position
While offering their profiles
Like notables at a spa
Grouped for the lens.

They have settled into age
With a fear of being alone.
Such gaunt tranquillity,
A herded peace!

You stand at its foot
A mere nanunculus,
Or whisper at its brow
An imprecation

Which the wind removes,
Whisked into the air
With all your vanity,
A minor annoyance

Not to be compared
With trigonometry,
Telescopes, masts, picnics
Or the puncture of flags.

Or that old enemy
Who at his leisure reduces
Outcrop to random rocking
Impedimenta.

For as you slither down
The mossed escalation
Of shifting lichen-wrapped
Smashed crocks

A vertical wall to your right
Unbelievably still
And staunch to its terrain,
A ruinous piping

You see what brings you down
Fear stroking the scalp:
Not mere height or exposure
Or being alone

But the dawning role of invader
Animated, flushed, hostile,
Conspirator and wrecker,
Almost indecent.

Up there are old mysteries
Much better left alone,
Safer with our structures
Of docile stone.

2

They own everything,
Saddled with foot-thick wool
And a family resemblance
Like the first Marlboroughs.

Inquisitive and alarmed,
Their slit eyes blank
As undone buttonholes,
They circle the cottage.

To them it memorialises
Worlds of purpose and concept
Unhabitable, like
A stone footprint.

How we come in and out
Is certainly a puzzle
For there they are, puzzled,
Whenever we do it.

Grouped on frosty nights
When with a cautious beam
We tread into the black
Their eyes are green.

And on misty mornings
Moving like ancient sofas
On castors over the gravel
They keep their watch.

For the mountain is edible.
Its small geography
Is their prerogative:
Their paths are meals.

They might even admit
To being its parasites,
As they have parasites
Nuzzling richly.

But what of a creature
Who lives not by the grass
But by the hidden stone,
Its skeleton?

Not as the tasteless crag
Or scrambling sideways scree
Whose dangers are well-known
But a shut cave

In which unspeakable acts
Of gregariousness and greed
Or of sheer stupidity
Are hidden from them?

They may, though bewildered,
Secretly guess our kinship,
Nomads to them and less
Aristocratic.

This would certainly account
For their intermittent patience,
Explain why we feel just
A little sheepish.

3

She makes a quick escape
As from a cold cauldron,
Seeping frugally but
In slight panic

Moistening sheer outcrop
With tears of brave joy,
Long legs down the rock,
A flicker of lace.

Just a slip of a girl
But something to be proud of
Elbowing thorns and stones
And growing stronger

Talking at roadsides where
A small declivity
A tumble of clod and pebble
Whitens her falling

Rushing on in excitement
Through a fledgy wood,
Dropping helter-skelter
Flirting with fish

Lingering in pools
Where hardly visible flies
Have just time enough to cast
A static shadow

And moving down the hillside
Through half-flooded meadows
Where thirsty herds make for
The tell-tale hummocks.

Soon her progress is statelier
On the reed-crowded route
Under footpath and bridge
To her dissolution.

We admire this quality
Of drawing out as on
A thread an argument
Of pure persistence

Until diversity
Sinks with delicious freight
The empty tanker of
Our finite voyage.

For see: the ravine holds her
Where sun-worshippers trudge
With all their full baskets
To the earth's lap.

Whereupon she promptly
Disappears, spilled
Out to random skeins
Across the beach

Rejoining, without complaint,
The globe's great cycle
As who would not wish to do
Did we not stop here?

4

For this is what it comes down to:
After repose, erosion.
From grandeur, detonations
And heartless breakdown.

But if this were the way
We died into the earth
Think of the discretion,
Such privacy!

Privacy of worlds
Not wasted but perpetual,
Tons and tons of indifference,
Lightness of heart.

Grain by grain it offers
Little resistance, only
Corporate mass and that
Agreeably wayward.

Wet, it preserves the wraith
Of toes. Dry, it dissolves
The tread to dredged craters
Lodged with beer-cans.

The loose configurations
Of this sterile humus
Are without finitude:
Frankly, a mess.

Its yellowness is false,
A lie to anger the blue
Which hammers arms and fists
In tears against it.

For down there the chiselled specks
Are proud of their lineage:
Crystal, tan, charcoal,
Their colours are sober.

Flushed by the watery beast
They assert their freedom
In voluntary association,
A righteous rebuttal.

Good reason to admire, then,
The ultimate in stone
Neither to be climbed nor hewn,
The body's haven.

For here we face our star
With least speculation,
Here we are revolved
In certainty.

Here warmth is transmitted.
Your idle hand reaches
And grasps a myriad boulders
Of impossible size.

As they bounce off the palm
Like sparks from a welder
Your hand seems invulnerable.
Colossal. Painless.

CAIRN

Stairs leading nowhere, roof
To no accommodation, monument
To itself, half-scattered.

An old badge of belonging
To the available heights,
A shrug and a smile, as though

Having climbed two thousand feet
You could climb a few feet more
And the view might be different.

WILD RASPBERRIES

Wild raspberries gathered in a silent valley
The distance of a casual whistle from
A roofless ruin, luminous under sprays
Like faery casques or the dulled red of lanterns
When the flame is low and the wax runs into the paper,
Little lanterns in the silence of crushed grasses
Or waiting chaises with a footman's lights,
Curtains hooked aside from the surprising
Plump facets padded like dusty cushions
On which we ride with fingers intertwined
Through green spiky tunnels, the coach swaying
As it plunges down and the tongues slip together,
The jewels fall to the floor to be lost forever,
The glass shatters and the heart suddenly leaps
To hear one long last sigh from an old blind house
That settles further into its prickly fronds,
Speaking of nothing, of love nor of reproaches,
Remembering nothing, harbouring no ghosts,
Saving us nothing at all but raspberries.

HUT GROUPS

On these small eminences above the valley
So hugged by excited bracken from which the wind
Enforces obedience that their very insignificance
Seems a quiet triumph, their demise an unfortunate
Accident reversible through incantations or simple good will,
On these the hidden foundations stand of the Dark Age farms,
Their slight turfy bulk squaring a hillside or a field.

An eight-figure map reference will find them
Though they are less visible than an overnight
Encampment of moles. Where even their simple doors were
Can't be rumbled through the attentions of the illegible grass.
You may stand in them as the sheep do and not feel at home,
And yet delight in the mere persistence of a habitable shape,
A ground-plan of biographies which might yet be relived.

We have stood in our own foundations, haven't we,
And marvelled at the exiguous dimensions? Later,
Closed from the elements and their whining questions
By the courtesy of a roof and walls that seem solid enough,
We may cheerfully forget our portion of earth and its location.
While we are alive we may hold each other in three dimensions,
Safe from the wind and, miles down underfoot, the turbulent
     weed.

What shadows we cast, what infirmities and endurance,
What ghosts we send stumbling up ivory keys in deserted rooms
Or sobbing from scenes of defeat too shameful to be
     remembered,
What touch implanted carelessly or with fondness on skin and
     stem
Which hold their parley with oblivion and the encircling air
Can so establish the certainty of our distinctiveness
As these can time's hunger? None, I think.

DUG BUTTONS AND PLATES

The hill is on the move, grass to be scraped
Again from cobbles, bridles where they lay
Now dug from inches under, shirts leaving
Their skeletons of buttons, hostages
To contours only perceptibly the same.

Crouching with trowels we are moved by these
And by the swallows and blue bridges of
A commonplace mosaic, lost fragments
On which again the leaves and shoots might steam
Did not the blackened edges interrupt.

All the dead meals dwindle to their seeds,
Cuffs unfastened and rolled back for the heat,
The spade working not at random but in rows,
Sweat wiped on forearms and the soil lying
Choiceless, uneager, for what it will receive.

These buttons will not grow. The shape-echo
Lives only backwards, to hands unbuttoning,
The act forgotten, pearl and bone sucked thin.
But come, let us gather them for this reminder:
The drill of seeds, the hill coming down.

EVENING SIGNS AT GALLT-Y-CEILIOG

Why here? Have we stopped pretending not to notice?
Glance up to the window: something has just disappeared.
Try to read, and find it clamouring for attention.

The house is establishing its relations with the hill,
Its corners not its sides at compass points,
The hill edging it out into the sun.

The evening chaffinch scours for basking grubs.
The long-shadowed flock squeeze their tattoos of dung
Like dropped jewels pattering on the gravel.

What does the house know, patient of all its creatures?
Patient of bird and sheep and the small movements
Of uncollected insects and the first bat?

It must be the hill's secret, older than the stones
Which make the spaces we furnish with our laughter
And chill the natural warmth of turf and spray.

The chairs are angled for conversation like
A stage set. A hand writes, detached and horrible.
One more bottle and the mountain will be level!

Why here? Is it something about to come or to go?
The house knows nothing, neither does the hill.
The creatures walk in their created shadows

Noiseless as the burning tread to the west of the sun
Returning from its career as a minor god,
Parting the sea, coming at last to land.

Why here? The meeting-place of all the made
And unmade, is it, a point of old discomfort?
The signs are upon us, friends. We've no roots here.

IN THE ROOM

A leg walked into a room.
A grubby plaster assisted
The bending of the knee.

A hand was seen closing a door
Or bunched over an eggcup,
Wild grasses and a smudge of harebell.

A foot offered itself for inspection
Beside an empty sandal. The long nail
Curled slowly away from the scissors.

For a moment the mirror contained a face
And the face looked back at itself,
Incurious but content, as at the first chapter
Of a book read for the second time.

BOUNDARIES

Trees have come up as far as they can
And stand about uncertainly.
Beyond the thistles of the last field
A stream rises, and a lane links
The few farms.

Maps show the contours of the clays
And fields the justice done to heirs.
Down in the village the stream is boastful
Though it does nothing much up here.
You can walk across it.

Boundaries are what link us, surely,
When neighbours turn together from barren
Pasture, when new walls remember
The passing of patriarchs, the drying
Of shared waters.

As trees send saplings to the valley
And all the lanes wind down again,
As the sun rises and sets, creating
New shadows from the same stone,
We are all one.

Within the exact boundaries of
Our skins, of which one inch beyond
Is Nomad's Lodge, the shivering crevice,
We create friend, daughter, lover.
The map converges.

SLEEPING OUT AT GALLT-Y-CEILIOG

Something, perhaps an idea, is again eluding me.
It belongs nowhere in particular but might
At any moment appear and surprise me.

It's not part of the usual epiphanies.
It has no colour, or even night-colour, since
Lying awake half the night will not fix it.

The trees are alive, the candle flame gusty
And flattened. We lie in our quilted chrysalises
With still heads, like ancient funeral masks.

The moon at our backs rises over the mountains:
An understudy, practising with silent lips,
Sharing the sky with one star above the holly tree.

Nothing is spoken. The precise text of leaf
And crag is not known, or has been quite forgotten.
We're happy with what is offered, like visitors.

Perhaps after all there is nothing to remember
But this simplicity. The grass is grey
At dawn. It is the earth awakes, not I.

MORNING

Again the curlew rehearses
His rising liripoop
And the shepherd walks up there
In the shadow of the early sun.

Here is the gate which still
Is icy-cold to the touch
With memories of all mornings
In a short share of time.

These long low whistles
Stroking the humped hills
Are like old spells for waking
The unbroken light.

Now a celebrant cock
With fantasies for news
Locates a distant farm
With a strangled dignity.

A hand on a gate is enough
To thrill through to the bone
With love for such strange sounds
And for a still sleeping house.

Ear, eye and hand
At once precise and blurred.
Dew handprints on iron.
The valley filled with mist.

WALKING BELOW CARN GUWCH

It's going fast. Old roads
Are green again and gates
Tied up. The little church
Shares its field with a blind
Congregation of straggling
Mushrooms. Below, the river
Bends as we expect it
To, attended by curlews
That no map needs to show.

It's going fast and we
Will never find it once
It's gone. Not in stone
Or surprising photographs,
Not in handwriting
Or careful recipes.
Far from our sealed diseases
We sense it in the river
And the sadness of the curlews.

It's going fast. Somehow
It rises on the wind,
A metamorphosis
Of an idea pursued
Until it took quick fright.
The bodies of the children
Are budding, an old response
Which says: It's our world now
And going on forever.

MUSHROOMS

Elusive to our spells, these chambers
Tented in grass: we stoop and plod
About the church insanely, like penitents.

White and soft as conjurors' gloves,
Edging like eggs or ears out
Of the field's moist green table.

Wedded with fine hairs to a mystery
They part from when tugged like a plaster,
The thumb stump delicately clogged with soil.

Frightening, the exuded tips and domes!
But still we search and pick, our baskets
Smelling fragrantly of underground caverns.

It's as though if we left them they would bud
Into faces and not, as we know, grow skirts
Which drop to a black lace as the air melts them.

VOICE AND EYES

Pleased at an unknown bird,
A custom or a trade,
As for a moment the voice
Falters and the hands
Are masterful, or eyes
Move upwards to the mountain
And conversation stops.

Quiet when listening,
Or at a familiar task,
As in a wood a voice
Calls, a shape among
The leaves, or eyes
Stray over the bushes
Sprung with the weight of bees.

Alone and conscious of it,
Or waiting to be met,
As from the cliff a voice
Returns upon itself
In laughter, or eyes
Look down the lane at nightfall
For the eyes coming up.

FIRE ON THE BEACH

The wrinkled web between
The thumb and finger
Is where hands meet,
Lizard hinge that makes
A magnet of the skull
And the heart race.

Such diplomacy
Can scarcely guard us
From greater intimacy,
Palm containing palm
Lifted slightly like
A letter guessed for weight.

Beacon to no ships
Its purpose is to burn
All that will burn,
Consuming every plank
And furred splinter,
Raising tar to a froth.

We stagger round it
In a comfortable stupor,
Raking the tideline
For the unlikeliest offerings:
Nets, dolls, feathers,
Great wigs of weed.

Now it cracks pebbles like eggs
Where once with cautious hand
We held out only what
The flame could bear to touch,
Thin stuff, stripped by the sea
But dry enough to catch.

CAER ARIANRHOD

A village in the sea! The map says that
Tradition says so, barely casting doubt
On the gaze and gossip of those generations
For whom a map could never end at the shore
Where livelihood begins, that salt harvest
To be shared with busts of seals who come to dine
Alone, like emperors, in the black waves.
Or with ghosts that the sea claimed from time to time
As at low tide upon a summer's night
A homeward boy tugging his skiff across
The calmed surface saw lights and shapes down there
Like faces of strangers in doorways looking out
Through unremembered evenings, and not a cry
To break the silence of the flood but the small
Pirate clink of the rowlocks at the pull of the oars
And the boat's terrified speed over the roof of the sea.

ANNIE UPSIDE DOWN

What a position! I might as well be dead
 And suspended in the sea,
My feet treading the blue laid out beneath my head
 Like infinity.

I never thought the sky could press so hard
 Or rock needed my hair
As roots for the blood to pound through, with my feet starred
 Against the air.

It's the whole earth turned inside out like a sock
 And me just hanging on.
It's no more than a sixpenny magnet: give me a knock
 And I'd be gone!

Didn't they use to bury you upside down?
 I've felt like this in a cellar
Bending for coal. But then I wasn't snagged like a clown
 Or a wounded umbrella.

It's the wire that's got me as it pinches wool.
 Isn't there someone coming
Whistling up the mountain for sheep who could give me a pull?
 My head is drumming.

Once from bits on fence and thorn I wove a
 Skirt, something for free.
Retaliation! There never was a wall I couldn't get over:
 Now it's got me.

Where are Owl and Hugh, those gentle boys
 With deep pockets and a stone
For the dark pool in the wood where the eels made no noise
 Swimming alone?

How I ran after that pair just to be taught a
 Way to catch fish, and froze
As they held me by the bare heels with my hands in the slimy
 water,
  Tickling my toes!

Harry Tidy and Peter Shape would grin
　　To see me on my head,
Who keep their balance as they keep their money in
　　A feather bed.

And poor Tim Molehouse who for a whole spring
　　Called to me from the garden
Might beg not for my finger for his mother's ring
　　But for my pardon.

Why should he think it sinful not to marry?
　　As if I belonged to him
One bit more than I belonged to Peter or Harry.
　　Unhappy Tim!

There's many in their farms have shut their doors
　　When I walked down the hill,
Though never did I once look back or without cause
　　Wish them ill.

God help them with their sanctimonious drivel!
　　They shall be stunned as an ox is
And shovelled into the black field under slabs that swivel
　　Like pencil-boxes.

There let them gape as they have gaped from birth
　　And gaping let them rot,
Each open mouth a rim of bone clogged up with earth
　　Like a buried pot.

The soil shall not take me, caught up in my snare
　　Like an old hanged ferret.
I am for the sun and the dissolving wind: the air
　　Shall inherit.

I must weigh more than I thought. If I had wings
　　I wouldn't be in this mess,
Slumped in the sack of my body and gloomily thinking of things
　　To hate and confess.

Just like the redstart building I'd be gone
　　With a moment on the stone
To check my heartbeat and an eye for danger. One
　　Is too much alone

Where pairs are rooted. Clumsy arms and legs
    May be love's second-best,
But look how wings brave gravity to lower eggs
    Into the nest!

I saw the tell-tale twigs on precipices:
    Amazing! But why therefore
Should *I* be fastened to the tilted hill with kisses
    I did not care for?

I've had my arms round necks I saw too clearly
    For any kind of rapture:
No passing longing for the ordinary is really
    Worth the capture.

Rather avoid it. Single as the peak
    Which every restless eye
Strays to when valleys are damp there's nothing that I seek
    More than the sky.

Faces in rooms have too much of their own
    Individual life,
Never the same when you look again, silently grown
    Hard as a knife.

I've flown in dreams so perfect they'd convince
    Me I might really try to
Waking, if only the old earth didn't say: 'Why, since
    You've nowhere to fly to?'

I have no wings but only this dead skirt
    Peeled back like a glove
As once I had when I was young and nothing hurt
    So much as love.

The years fall out of your pockets, something comes in
    To your head like a passing thought
And can't be set to rights once it's got inside your skin.
    There: you're caught.

Hitched to the ribs of a field like so much mutton
    It's a wonder the crows don't come.
I might have thought of somehow trying to undo a button
    But my arms are numb.

Now I have had enough. It's all very well
     To hang here for a time.
At first I could have laughed: head over heels pell-mell
     Like a pantomime!

Let me be upright now and take a bow.
     Where's my fairy queen
To wave her wand and say that she understands just how
     Patient I've been?

Surely someone will come and fetch me and gather
     Me up and set me down
And all the escaped sheep will come running with their blather
     From their green town?

And the mountain will surely swing back in a while
     To point in the right direction
And I stagger about on the grass with a dizzy smile
     At my resurrection?

Surely the air after all this time has kept
     One secret, however old?
I can almost hear it, and I would stay to hear it except
     I am very cold.

Just a whisper would do it, the wind among
     The branches where we stood
Once listening for the mouse's and the eel's tongue
     In the dark wood.

Or water falling as if for all time
     Out of the rock, so cool
And calm the silent threads seemed almost to climb
     From pool to pool

And the eye moving upwards to lose that downward sense
     And all the elements weave in
A strange stillness and mysterious excellence
     I could believe in.

Such a secret would be worth the wait
     As birdsong after a night
Of horrors. There's hope for things to happen, though too late.
     And they might. They might.

TWO VOICES

'Love is a large hope in what,
Unfound, imaginary, leaves us
With a beautifying presence.
Love always grieves us.'

So sang youth to the consenting air
While age in deathly silence, thus:

'Love is a regret for what,
Lost or never was, assails us
With a beautifying presence.
Love never fails us.'

SONG FOR A CONDEMNED QUEEN

Shall you revisit as ghost or shadow
This world of waters that you wept?
Shall you revisit, though it be narrow,
The bed of tears your weeping kept?
We smooth the creases in your pillow
    Where you have slept.

Silver glitters in the furrow
Where the lost coin records your name.
Winter fastens clod and harrow
And a cloistered queen the same.
Though ice describes the grassy meadow
    Your tears remain.

Shall you revisit as winter's fellow,
Shut in his coldness with your fame?
Shall you come startled to the window,
Finding frost-flowers upon the pane?
They will remind you of your sorrow
    And turn to rain.

Though the world sink again we follow
The pain and patience of your love.
Though waters spread they will be shallow.
Familiar hills will peep above.
You will return like the shot arrow,
    Like the first dove.

THE DUKE'S PAGODA

Tomorrow I will order stones
Beside a lake that is the shape
Of all desire, the lengthened ace
Unshadowed by its border,
No rose to break the perfect rim
Or water falls from wall to wall
To veil the cupolas and still
The single carp. And there
In tiers of rose and grey will rise
A wedding of Greece and China
From which the landscape seems to fall
As stair by stair turns round.
And nothing could be finer than
The way the walks direct the eye
To each of the six corners,
While from the topmost balcony
Showing like trumpets through the trees
The towers of Amboise will be seen
In the still hours of grey and green.

It stands in peace where once were nests.
Lights flicker in avenues
Where I can walk about, and then
About again, towards the stones.
It will suffice to turn my thoughts
Upwards, though at the pinnacle
Where can I look but down? And down
Again, and down the turning stairs
Must at the end of perfect days
Walk. The hills are lit
Beyond the window slits that turn,
Movement in stillness like a love
For everything unknown, and I
Still exiled with a summer frown,
The evening birds against my ear
Secure in leafy thrones.
All sullen beauty may be charmed
By the mysterious blood of building.
Tomorrow I will order stones.

THE WILDERNESS

A memory of Oscar Silverman in Buffalo, 1962

Displaying a wicked smile through his morning cigarette
Like a benign Demon King wistful for home-cooking,
Smiling his big smile of seduction and authority,
Oscar said: 'Today I'm going to give them *Henry IV*
And you can be Hal. Can't you?' I supposed I could be.

Yes, I was Hal. And Oscar ceased for an hour to be
Professor of English and Chairman of the Department.
He sat on a desk and chatted to the Seniors,
His charm unwearied, his enthusiasm without reserve,
The big collapsed roué's visage alive with naughtiness.

And Shakespeare's dialogue confirmed their impression
Of a visiting stranger in an armour of self-control,
Wrapped in his own atmosphere of curiosity and judgement
With an alien humour and a palpable timidity:
I was a useful assistant and the old man's foil.

Fifteen years ago it was easy to be the empirical Hal.
I was angler and non-swimmer on the bank of that river
Which shifts us so slowly but certainly along, noting:
'I believe the wilderness will be new to all the party.
The Miss Bertrams have never seen the wilderness yet.'

As though we really were required to escape being in character,
As though life were designed to parade its ridiculous threats,
Like a sober doom, at once glamorous, sedate and sinister!
And there was a justice in the role I played, endorsing
A poetry of implication, disturbance and restraint.

They told me it was the coldest place in America, and sure
    enough
A colleague got frostbite just walking across the car-park.
In the year of the Cuban missiles, under campus ivy I wrote:
'The wilderness is what we see from broken shades.'
But I was secure as Pope 'descending' to the gaieties of Horace.

I had located a role for the broken city about me
Like the Lisbon earthquake, sitting in our green apartment
On the corner of LeBrun and Winspear, not explaining myself,
Dreaming in the prose style of Gibbon of the violent landscape,
Ice crusting the trees, cars smashing in the streets.

But Oscar, that kindly master of the academic ceremonies,
Had something else to tell me if I had listened.
There is a life of all lives to be lived that will contain us,
That draws us to its centre with no kind of calculation,
Native, beyond art and of a power to forgive our rejection.

It is without honour, no punched card or map of it
Exists to be consulted and the city has not heard of it.
It has never been rehearsed and cannot be explained,
And though you may begin to define it by knowing the
     wilderness,
Its easy habits may well take a lifetime to learn.

And so he must have known as he sat on the edge of the desk,
Betraying confidences like a shopper in a tea-room,
Giving assurances like a doctor with his bag on the bed,
Appealing for support like a crafty baby with a toy:
The students listened, as did his ignorant accomplice.

'A goodly portly man, i'faith, and a corpulent;
Of a cheerful look, a pleasing eye, and a most noble carriage.'
Here was a humour indeed, a man confronting the wilderness,
Knowing the good places to eat, guardian of the wonderful
     papers,
His two daughters, and the many kinds of apple.

WELL SAID, DAVY

He went to the city and goosed all the girls
With a stall on his finger for whittling the wills
To a clause in his favour and Come to me Sally,
One head in my chambers and one up your alley
    And I am as old as my master.

I followed him further and lost all my friends,
The grease still thick on his fistful of pens.
I laced up his mutton and paddled his lake
In the game of Get-off-me and Just-for-my-sake
    And I am as old as my master.

I sang in his service a farewell to sorrow
With rolled black stockings, the bone and the marrow.
The Law was a devil to cheat as you pleased
As we knelt on the backs of the city girls' knees
    And I am as old as my master.

So back to the country where birds are squawking,
With possets for pensions and witless talking
Of walloped starvelings and soldiers' fortunes
From his nodding bench in the smothered orchards
    And I am as old as my master.

Age turns the cheek of a buried scandal
In a nightmare of cheese and a quarter of candle.
When the servant is privy he's good as a guest,
The first to be carved to and last to be pressed
    And I am as old as my master.

Country or city, no pleasure can last:
It's farewell to the future and beckon the past.
Though he that we drink with is sometimes a fool,
A single grey tooth may furnish a smile
    And I am as old as my master.

THE KISS

Who are you,
You who may
Die one day,

Who saw the
Fat bee and
The owl fly

And the sad
Ivy put out
One sly arm?

Not the eye,
Not the ear
Can say Yes:

One eye has
Its lid and
Can get shy;

One ear can
Run out and
Off the map;

One eye can
Aim too low
And not hit;

One ear can
Hug the air,
Get too hot.

But lip and
Red lip are
Two and two,

His lip and
Her lip mix
And are wed,

Lip and lip
Can now say:
'You may die

But not yet.
Yes, you die
But not yet.'

The old lie.

IN THE CORRIDOR

Francis, it *was* you yesterday, though I knew you were dead,
     Smiling and nodding your head
As though your long-kept secret could wait a little while
     To be recounted in style,
Fondly amused at my pain and excitement at seeing you there,
     At seeing you anywhere
When I thought, when I knew, the historical you that really
     mattered
          Had been so cruelly scattered.
It must have been you I recognised as much as the once alive,
     Unless those who survive
Go on and on as they did investing the shapes of friends
     For their own strange ends
With the voice and significance of what affects them most.
     Like an over-insistent host,
'Francis, what *happened*? Tell me. Tell me how you escaped'
     I silently mouthed and gaped,
Eager and simple for a startling truth. I was so compelled
     To what seemed to be withheld
That I moved along the corridor towards your stillness
     As doctors deal with illness,
Reckless of answers that the only cure requires,
     Immune to its desires.
But of course the darkness shielded you from inquisition
     And I froze in the position
Of one whom the dead night's noiseprint has suddenly caught
     awake
          Like one frog in a lake
When all else is slow mist rising to meet the moon
     And the first light all too soon
Shocks us to a reappraisal of that brief deep
     And self-satisfied sleep
Which is our charmed life. In the corridor
     My bare feet on the floor
Were rooted even as I thought I began to tread
     In drawn and willing dread
The several thousand and worn stitches that lay between,
     Its invisible brown and green.

You will forgive, I am sure, that craven breaking of the spell
    Though you may have wished to tell
Secrets that only such silence and respect of fear
    Ever allow us to hear.
Francis, now I have seen you once more, knowing you are dead,
    Though nothing at all was said,
I know that for you the future has ceased at all to exist
    And will not be much missed.
Only our sorrow for you will come again and again
    And goes some way to explain
Why there is fit passage for its evidence of our fears
    In a few words and tears.

THE MOST DIFFICULT POSITION

– Wer mit dem Leben spielt,
Kommt nie zurecht;
Wer sich nicht selbst befiehlt,
Bleibt immer ein Knecht.
(If you think life's a game
You'll never get anywhere;
Lose your self-control
And you'll always be a slave.)

(Goethe)

1 *Staunton prologises*

(Spring, 1858)

Now mind those papers with your pretty foot!
They may not seem in order, but they are:
The order of the mind at least, the mind
That stacks the evidence with faultless art.
Dead king. Wicked uncle. Mad prince. Queen
Unusually weak, ambiguous.
I speak now of the Bard. The trick's the same:
To link the salient facts organically.
You see my labours at their deepest here,
With analogues from Scandinavian myth
And penny fables. I'm too proud to tread
The pitons of the frozen commentators?
Fair charge, not true. They're harbingers, not rivals.
I map what they surmised and at a stroke
I free the ice-bound glacier of their text
Till all is moving river, warm and full.
That's Theobald you tread on, Whiter you clutch
As though to dub me silent to your service!
My dear, I'm sorry. Something in your look
Speaks of a small offence, and yet you smile
Despite yourself. I like to talk to you,
Rare visitor, as Gertrude will not talk,
Nor talked to Theobald nor Whiter neither,
Whom you may now put down. He cost me much
To find. What is it, dear? Is that the time?
Well, well, I see. Is dinner cold? I'm sorry.

A fruitful morning swollen to a day
And like to drop untasted. I've worked well
But work's a tyrant. My edition grows
An ogre's task, eating up time and life;
Truth's straws for spinning into gold,
An ogre's task without the lucky ring,
Though you, dear, are my ring, and golden too
To help me shift the straws, defeat the ogre.
       I saw you in the garden through the window
Reaching for roses. You sustain my labours
As the bright stream an oak that arches over.
Thought in your presence is a growing silence
That feeds invisibly upon my love.
(Pass me my cigars: you will not mind?
Thank you. It helps me to unwind my thoughts.)
I have been thinking for an hour on end
About the guilt (or innocence) of Gertrude,
Who had no time for roses, and was weak.
Strange that the ivory there, the red and white,
How strange that in her realm of four and sixty
Small distinct dominions the queen
Is most powerful! Did Shakespeare play the game?
Undoubtedly. And missed his dinner too,
Writing his high and witty heroines
Whose power lay in their tongues. (Another match:
The leaf is unwilling to admit the fire.
Sit down, too, and be patient. I will come
To sift the prandial leavings soon enough.)
       Time tells all, backwards as well as forwards,
Turns stage to altar and the luscious hybrid,
Static in crystal vases, to a nomad;
Chequered applewood and trailing hems
To our nude parents; and the ivory *vierge*
There by your elbow to a Persian *firz*,
Proud Amazon to greybeard counsellor.
When my edition's done, I may find time
To write a paper on the piece's role,
Its history and curious change of sex.
Yes, it would please me to explore the case,
But time's my tyrant, as you know, my dear.
If I could queen my hours into years!

I have my public and my publishers
Hot on my neck; the endless correspondence,
Friendly analysis of my past games
With Anderssen (the gross presumption of it!),
Offers to play, requests for information,
The search for books; the endless annotation,
Feeding the *Illustrated London News*,
My all-devouring column; queries from Routledge,
Hints of the advance and long delay.
It never stops. Look at this letter here.
It came this morning. No, you didn't see it.
You had that letter from your Indian cousin
If you remember. The New Orleans Chess Club,
I quote: 'The undersigned committee has
The honour to invite you to our city
And there meet Mr Morphy in a chess match.'
(Do they think that I could take the boat tomorrow?)
'We see no valid reason why an exercise
So intellectual and ennobling is
Excluded from the generous rivalry
Found between the Old World and the New
In every branch of human industry.'
(Pompous asses!) 'It unfortunately happens
That serious family affairs prevent
Mr Morphy from entertaining, for the present,
The thought of visiting Europe.' (Mummy won't let him!)
'The amount of the stakes, on either side, to be
Five thousand dollars.' Five thousand dollars?
Really, my dear, it is intolerable.
Does the boy think that life all over Europe
Can grind to a halt merely to give him the pleasure
Of sitting and facing his elders and betters over
A Lilliputian army of carved ivory?
          You smile, do you? Am I unreasonable?
You think I should be gracious and consent?
That I am world champion and can afford to?
Am I world champion, then? Am I indeed?
Don't you imagine that Mrs Anderssen
Is saying just the same today to him
And over the very same letter? Oh yes, I know
That I was out of practice when he beat me,
The grinning schoolmaster from frozen Breslau!

'Poor Staunton was out of practice.' It was a mistake
And I shall not repeat it. I am a scholar
And my work comes first. Five thousand dollars!
Someone somewhere hopes to make some money!
Morphy's games are very pretty but
They will not bear the test of analysing.
(My cigar is out again.) He's just a child!
A child beginning a career of conquest!
More like Barnum and Bailey's three-ringed circus
With General Tom Thumb and other wonders.
What does the drum beat and the billboard say?
That Morphy played in the cradle; scorned his books,
Guessing the gambits as Newton knew his Euclid,
By intuition: beat Löwenthal at thirteen
And Paulsen in New York last year; recites
Unfalteringly from his memory
The entire Civil Code of Louisiana,
And what not else? With such politeness too,
The newsmen marvelling: 'Mr Paulsen never
Makes an oversight; I sometimes do.'
A circus! Am I to put on greasepaint then
And tumble for the eager multitude?
Would you like me to? You think it important?
You see me as your valiant Perceval?
　　　　Important? My dear, consider. Please don't mistake me.
The game of chess is supremely unimportant:
As, shall we say, a trellis of climbing roses
Watered and cut by a sweet and gloveless lady
(Now, now! Don't hide it! Give me your tender scratches
So I may make a handy sandwich of them.
There, hidden in mine and healed by love!
I thrive upon such spiritual dining).
The game of chess is unimportant as
The exercise of dogs or whisker-wax,
Hot meat brought level in with steady wrists,
A letter from a cousin in Jodhpur
With talk of franchise and a sale-of-work.
You see? It neither does nor does not matter.
A rose is beautiful, the meat gets cold
Or eaten, the cousin relieves her loneliness,
The dogs are healthy. So is my moustache.

Thus the queen moves this way or that way, thus
She is sacrificed, no more or less a queen
Than that in stone and sepia, two removes
From the banality, work of the box
And chemicals and ineffable loyalty
Of the Jodhpur cousin. Don't take away your hand!
I'm not teasing. It's true. Don't you see?
I love it. It's delightful and it's moral.
Its mimic battles are engaged upon
For neither prize nor honour. It's a game
For Aristotle not for Perceval
So how should it be used for a career?
        I'll show you what I mean. We'll play together,
You and I, as lovers used to do
In Europe's maytime. Push the board between us.
It's white and red, a contest like the roses.
I'll give you knight and rook, and you begin.
Every little lathing sings of the stage
Now, doesn't it? You see the fascination.
The happy warrior pops out like a sparrow
Quick under the blossoming may and steady,
His head small and alert upon its ruff.
There on the lawn, you see one? He's pretending
The philopluvial bisexuals can
Escape him, one eye out for the dangerous rival.
A page or two, attendant on the king?
Slight and foppish? Yes, but watch that worm!
The throat moves. A glove's or fan's adjusted.
Some grand theme is broached. Do you hear the words?
No matter. The scene changes. Sir Something's bold
To make a broil, raise an old quarrel or
Concoct an accusation of a sort.
Familiar story. Anything will do.
Sir Other's at him, and the pages freeze,
Locked face to face. The Sirs are at a distance
But engaged. Is it the Quiet Game?
You have me waiting. Thorns' stigmata hover
Above the board. I'm in my heaven now.
It's an age-old theatre that nature knows
And mounts each year not thinking of expense.
Infinite shapes! Tautologies of flowers!
Is it the Quiet Game? You like the Scotch.
I'd wager for the Scotch, a safe good game.

Your eye is sparkling, though. You know how custom
Stales. In moves your bishop like a cruet!
Down to Knight Five: that gives it flavour, just
A taste of risk. But can you see it through?
I never like to play this opening
Named for the sage advice of Ruy Lopez
In his *Libro del Arte del Juego del Axedres*:
Too much decisiveness too early here
And larger birds, their beaks festooned with worms,
May fly to freedom from their ravening.
But still, you see the life of the thing. My point
Is that it *is* like life, supremely so,
And all the world's a stage. The entrances
And exits finely done. Above all, exits!
Bishops arraign the weak Plantagenet,
The queen has vigorous notions of her own,
The old knight blusters, humoured by a boy
Who is not ignorant of the eighth square.
Plantagenet retires into his castle,
The queen has executions to arrange,
The knight must go. Yes, going out is all.
So many ways of going, many deaths.
The beak stabs suddenly like this, my dear,
And look: I have your pawn here in my hand,
Bald as a baby and as helpless, too.
As helpless as a worm. So many ways:
The boast, the whimper and the silent prayer,
The brute resistance and the daring feint,
The outraged protest and the resignation,
Self-slaughter, sui-mate, the noble gesture.
So many ways, and Shakespeare knew them all.
I understand it, or at least I try to.
I've mastered what I can. I am respected.
It is the game I love and not success.
Five years ago I challenged any comer
And no one came, not even Anderssen.
Now comes this boy, this Morphy. Shall I wait
On him? I think not. Shall I jump to the challenge
Of a boy with the face of a young girl in her teens?
I decline. I have a significant position.
I am Howard Staunton, I believe that I am happy.
The sun is low and strikes across the lawn
As the birds begin to sing. One crimson petal
Falls from your excellent roses. Your move, my dear.

2 Morphy persists

(Summer and Autumn, 1858)

Mother, you'll think I've not written before because I forgot to
Or maybe because in the end I only too well remember
Your tears at the quayside, your tears and your casual hurt
  exhortations,
Your tears at my firm uncancelled intention, your tears at my
  silence.
Yes, I remember it all and it seemed a fitting departure
For one who had vowed to defy such an elusive opponent.
Tears cover many regrets and emotion's a difficult subject,
Likely, I think, to defeat all but the most assiduous,
Likely to daunt any student with its impossible answers
To all the unknown questions. Ascribe a motive to weeping!
Might as well go to the Mississippi for a true confession
Or rifle the desert for clues to long-lost extravagant feelings.
Moisture flies up the offered cheek and the ducts receive it,
Kisses stagger back through the no-man's land of volition
Quite unhurt, though dazed and shocked and totally useless.
The *Arabia* hoots for the very last time and the hawsers are
  slackened.
There in the mind the dubious orders, checked and rechecked,
Yield not the slightest clue towards their interpretation.
Mother, I ask you: just what do you think you are losing?
Is it a dutiful son, or is it the wealthy attorney
You hoped perhaps I'd become if I persevered with my studies?
Have you examined the terms of that familiar equation?
Where is the unknown factor, the one that you've cancelled out?
Wouldn't success in itself give a more satisfactory answer?
Isn't it just the factor that all the terms contrive to
Shape to some kind of formulation, however clumsy?
Wouldn't success in this way be a relative sort of objective?
Not as a matter of pride, and certainly not of money,
But simply all by itself, being the common factor?
Well, neither is wholly true nor wholly false: I assert
Over the black and the white the exact ascendance of greyness.
That is something I fear they don't understand in New Orleans
Where questions of fact with the guns hang silently over the
  fireplace

And motive is whispered in fields or assassinated in ballrooms,
And pride is assigned to success, and weakness of course to
    failure
(Try telling Uncle Ernest to take a pride in failure!).
Can you honestly say that this disturbs and dismays you?
Mother, I ask you again: what do you think you are losing?
Is it my loss you fear, or might it be *my* losing?
If it were *that* I should smile, for it seems a fitting emotion
For one who has vowed to defy such a majestic opponent.
But, as I say, I find emotion a difficult subject.
That is of course my weakness, but weakness may lead to
    success,
For only a firm resolve and a singleness of purpose
Keep us applied to the matter in hand where feeling is stranger
And the mind runs even and smooth, oiled in a beautiful silence.
        Here in England, chess takes its proper place as a pastime.
It is not such a solemn affair, and yet, to be sure, it is serious.
Mother, I fear you could not understand the way it is taken,
Though sometimes when you sit at the piano I think you must
    know,
But if you know, you are silent, and silent most in talking:
There are some desperate silences when you're engaged in
    talking!
Hell. This looks like being another one of those letters
In which I say too much, – which I never get round to sending.
It's not so much a case of distance lending enchantment,
Licence to speak one's mind while the magic spell's unbroken;
Simply that such a perspective inclines one to see things clearly.
So must all travellers feel getting down at the end of their
    journey.
        For me, as you know, the event had a strange and
    significant meaning,
Liverpool sighted in patchy fog, June the twenty-first,
The *Arabia* docking at noon on the eve of my coming-of-age.
Newspapermen were not slow, I'm afraid, to remark on the date:
Did my parents object before, and was that the only reason
Why previously I had seemed unwilling to make the journey?
Facts, facts. What could I say? *Did* you give your consent?
I have to admit to myself that I really can't remember.
To the newspapermen I admitted the name of my hotel only,
Tired as I was and endlessly probed by their fatuous questions:
How many shirts did I have? Would I visit the opera?

That seventeenth move in my game in November with Paulsen,
Did I remember? Of course. The sacrifice of the queen.
I offered a clear and simple exchange of my queen for his bishop.
Paulsen was sure at the outset that it was a trap, cunning but
Obvious in a way, not one to easily fall for.
'Paulsen had worked out the combinations for six moves ahead,
      sir,
Six moves ahead! Taking an hour, and all the spectators
Excited and restless. An hour of thinking, and still couldn't see
      it.
Did he think you were mad, sir? He sat and he sat and he
      wondered
And took your queen. And the crowd gasped! And you said
      nothing.
Paulsen retired from the game at the end of eleven moves,
Eleven incredible moves ahead. Can you say, Mr Morphy,
What went on in your mind? Did you know? Had you worked it
      all out?
Or was it simply a stroke of luck, a leap in the darkness?'
      Silly to say that there's nothing to say, but it's true, there
      isn't.
All of us live in the dark, and many decline to leap
And so I knew that Paulsen would find it a deal of trouble.
Would it make news? I'd no idea, but I hoped it wouldn't.
News isn't really new but a long continuing process,
Daily refinement of what the readers have learned to expect.
Mine I have kept to the last, though you won't be thrilled to hear
      it.
Perhaps it won't absolutely displease you. It fills the paper,
And what is there else to do but to come to the end of the page,
The period which our pen proposes, or else turn over
To find that the sick white blank of the other side awaits us?
For pride is assigned to success, and weakness of course to
      failure,
And silence (how can we doubt it?) has nothing to do with
      feeling.
No, mother, I sign off here, and say: I have written to Staunton,
Written again to Staunton in the friendliest possible terms.
Can you in honesty say that this disturbs and dismays you?
How can it do that? No, I think you must wish me success,
But don't imagine it's pride that leads me on to the conquest.
No one who saw me now could ever think that it was.

*   *   *

No letters from home as yet, from you, or Helen, or Ernest,
But then there's nothing from Charles, and he would certainly
    write,
So I don't say this to rebuke but to damn the Atlantic packet
And to show how sick I am of the praise and the pearls and the
    parties.
Last night I heard Miss Louisa Pyne at the Philharmonic
In a pretty duet from the *Freischütz* before the Queen and Prince
    Consort:
Such idleness, such automatic applause before such beauty!
The English are superb, superb in their lack of thinking.
Quite early in the evening the gas went low and nearly
Disturbed the spectators' sleep with a fear of being left in the
    darkness,
Small drama, I know, but a real one, this fear of being left in the
    darkness.
Real like the fear of silence, the fear of the empty page.
To date I have written two, no three, plain letters to Staunton,
Three plain letters of challenge and always the same:
I will play you, he says, in September, in September or else in
    October.
I need just a few more weeks to brush up my openings and
    endings.
I will play you, he says, in October, in October or else in
    November.
        The curtain is rising for ever and the stage is always empty,
The rooms are impeccably dusted, the rooms with the lilies and
    roses,
The rooms that look out on the front, the rooms above
    Piccadilly,
The rooms in the feminine capital, the rooms of the Second
    Empire
(All good Americans when they die end up in Paris!),
The rooms all over Europe whose doors are incessantly opening,
Inviting the guest to flip open the well-filled silver inkwell,
To dip and relate with unaccustomed pen his travels.
All over Europe from room to room and always the same:
The doors are opening freely and the curtain is rising,
The sofas and chairs are placed just so, and the roses and lilies,
All the forwarded messages, cables and invitations,
And the little escritoire – there, in the right-hand corner!
Inviting the guest to record a transient name on the blotter,

Faint and reversed as the dreams he will dream on the single
   pillow.
Where is the action? Where is the speech and magnificent
   lighting?
Knuckles are still in repose at the end of my cuffs like tree-roots,
Springs of expensive clocks dilate in their glittering coils,
Visitors come and go on matters of no importance
And the curtain is rising for ever and the stage is always empty.

                        *   *   *

        That was a month ago already, and the letter's still with
   me.
Letters not sent assume a life of their own like monsters:
A sudden slow stare right into the gilt frame of the spirit
When only the eyes are seen but you know they belong to a
   stranger
And the memory can't be dispelled; it horribly lingers for ever.
The mouth is gaping open, the sickening flap unsealed.
You can't escape that singular moment of recognition:
Turn on the polished heel, fold back the unfolded paper,
But ever the haunting vision hovers over your shoulder,
Something that you created and will not let you ignore it,
A poor disfigured creature full of immortal longings,
A sort of ideal maimed by the uncontrolling hand,
A life that only endures as a vestige of what was intended.
Are we the same as we were, and will that be always the same?
My letter begins with rebukes, but that was a month ago,
A sloughed-off self in a limbo of lonely introspection.
That was already a month ago, and the letter's still with me.
I found it just now in a drawer with my socks in the hotel
   bedroom
And thought about what you had said of the praise and the girls
   and the parties,
And all my anger was gone when I came to the matter in hand.
At a distance all quarrels diminish and tend to resolve
   themselves into
A hard plain conglomeration of fact like a lawsuit.
But what is the law to say of the distance of space and time?
The law has nothing to do with time, as not of its making.
The law has nothing to do with space, for that it may break.

I felt today the first futility of the challenge
And all the sad impurities of life rose up together
As if to seize for themselves a prize that was not awarded,
And whiskered faces cheered, and no one was any the wiser.
    Can you imagine an afternoon in the north of England
In a flat damp August, sticky enough, but more dirty than
    sticky,
Walking across the Queen's College, Birmingham's brown
    narrow lawns?
On one side your true representative of modern American
    manners,
On the other the large *doyen* of large British Chess, Mr Staunton,
And as umpire Lord Lyttelton trotting, perspiring a little,
Blotting his face with a large chequered kerchief covered with
    pawns?
No one would try to keep the peace between two such as
Staunton and I seemed to be on that gloomy and brief occasion,
Only a man who had nothing to offer, and he had nothing.
'Howard?' he kept on saying, in a tone of interrogation
As close as it could get to an undemanding statement:
'Howard?' But Staunton, in the blandest possible manner,
Pausing only to lift a fading rose with one finger,
Talked without saying a thing, talked without making an
    answer,
Talked in a general way, smiled and was utterly charming.
'I will play you,' he said, 'in September, in September or else in
    October:
I need just a few more weeks to be clear of my other affairs,
Affairs of the greatest importance, I'm sure you understand.
What a delightful game! Delightful and scientific!
Scientific and moral, too, most moral of hobbies!'
    So it went on, and he forced me to feel the shame of
    persistence,
The squirming abject shame of inflicting myself upon him,
Taking his time and trying to hold him down to a promise;
Forced upon me the role of callow importuner
Seizing my chance to exploit a gentleman's casual interest,
Working with careful words and casual professional phrases
To lure him to some intense and somehow dangerous tourney;
Forced upon me the role of the eager smooth-talking gambler,
Cheeky at roadside inn or on Mississippi steamer;
Forced me to nod insanely at his procrastination:

'I will play you,' he said, 'in October, in October or else in
   November.'
What could I say? I felt I had somehow yielded a move for
Though in England chess takes its proper place as a pastime,
Though it is not such a solemn affair, it has its own logic,
And none in its deadly motions more practised than Howard
   Staunton,
Motions of serpentine skill and brazen prevarication,
Motions that know how they can afford to be lazily charming.
Lyttelton did his best, but his best was quite sadly useless:
November is merely a dream. The summer will fly like a winner,
Turf be untrodden, the crowds dispersed to their occupations.
Nothing can season the shocking taste of his blank refusal,
Nothing awaken him from his dream of victorious inaction,
Nothing disturb the unruffled surface of condescension,
The idle furloughs and barracks of a giant reputation,
The imperious posture of one who's unwilling to risk defeat.
I know it. And yet I hope. Hope against hope that sometime
The proud façade will crack, and light flood into the building.
But the curtain is rising for ever and the stage is always empty.

*   *   *

        To have no desires; worse, to have a desire for desires,
Is the death of the soul in its terrible grip of desiring to please.
Not the ideal, the burning ambition or even a hunger
For the trivial flush of content, the certain fact of fulfilment,
Simply the struggle to act one's part with the secret knowledge
That *this* is how it must be and nobody else may gainsay you.
How can I keep some sense of faith in my own objectives?
No one to trust, no one, and least of all the dragon
Roaring slightly again with his still-smouldering breath,
Saying at first he would only play in consultation,
Prowling about the tournament hall like a proud head-waiter,
Ready to offer advice to anyone he could rally,
Bland as a fighting bishop blessing the last battalion,
Lyttelton in despair, the Birmingham hotels full.
Now he announces his entry as quietly as he is able!
Staunton's decided to enter now that the lists are complete!
What's the idea? Does he want to storm his way through the
   talent,
Blaming a lucky accident if I manage to stop him,
Hoping I'll fall by chance to the Reverend Henry Salmon,
Hoping one way or another we'll never actually meet?

110

Credit will have to be given for such an adroit reversal
Coolly and casually made when nobody seemed to be looking!
    One thing is wrong with his plan, though: I shan't be there
    in person.
I wanted a private match, and the tournament doesn't amuse
    me.
Tomorrow I have proposed eight games without sight of the
    pieces,
Eight games together on Wednesday, sitting away from the
    tables.
Avery, Kipping and Wills, Rhodes, Carr and Dr Freeman
All have agreed with indecent haste to the blind encounter.
Lyttelton too will play, and the Reverend Henry Salmon.
Then I shall leave for Paris to see what *they* have to offer.
Anderssen will be there and others, perhaps, with manners.
Nothing is left for me here, at least until Birmingham's over.

*   *   *

    The curtain is rising still and the stage is always empty.
Why must we have a will when we don't know how to direct it?
Why must we have above all this dreadful desire for desires?
Where does the impulse come from? Do we acquire it, I wonder?
Or is it a secret alloy in the chain of bleeding that binds us
Fast to our foul perpetual history? Unwilling victims!
That I suppose was what in the first place moved me to study
How men have so arranged their affairs to make some kind of
    sense:
Power to do what the law allows is the only freedom.
Wriggling cells succumb to these ordered inventions of man, but
What is the law to say of the struggle of space and time?
The law has nothing to do with time, as not of its making.
The law has nothing to do with space, for that it may break.
Only the rules it energises, the rules and the fictions,
And I feel your heart across the sea making do with fictions,
For I sacrificed your strength for the sake of a wretched
    stalemate.
Some sort of brilliant sacrifice lies behind every challenge,
But to offer Andromeda up as a tasty bait for the dragon
And the dragon to turn up his nose: I can hardly bear to think it.
    At Birmingham, Staunton was out in the second round.
    Retiring
To Richmond to lick his wounds, he used his column to bait me.

111

It's clear we shall never play, and I will be home by Christmas.
And the *Illustrated London News* and the *New Orleans Delta*,
Even the *Birmingham Post*, will have to make do with fictions,
The fictions of law, the fictions of rules, the fictions of papers,
And the fictions of red and white, the thirty-two little fictions
Which have nothing to do with the heart, for that they may
    break
And what they break stands apart and watches in space and
    time
And I have failed you, mother, and cannot bear your look.
I have failed to kill the dragon, though Europe bows down before
    me.
I have failed to fulfil your strength, though Anderssen smiled in
    defeat
And deafened Paris suspected another revolution!
I have failed in the field of success, and my pride must give place
    to my weakness,
The weakness of wishing too much to engage in the pure world
    of mind,
Flickering light beyond the frowning behind the blindfold,
World where the thought rides on blood, instinctive in the
    darkness.
And what has the law to say of this fear of being left in the
    darkness?
What has the law to say of a son and his broken heart?

3 *Staunton epilogises*

(Spring, 1865)

    The desk is piled. Untired and regular
As mercury the level in trunk and stem
Rises, the old engagement, the old trumpets.
No question of anything different ever happening!
Those ducks on the lawn: every May they come
From their slowly moving home to a green slumber,
Heads tucked, dozing obliquely in marital content
Too far for snappishness or love's mirror-tricks
But close enough to have the air of posing
Like frugal boulders in that Kyoto garden
Perry reported, or perhaps a cannon at billiards.
All Nature mating with a *pion coiffé*!

Wasteful, prolific of rejected seeds
So one, the most unlikely, should win through.
And early roses just the same: trustful!
There will be frost, and you are far from here.
There will be frost, and nothing is the same.
Nothing can last, and everything is different.
I miss you! There's no one else to gather roses
And float them in silver dishes on the table.
Shutters are flapping. The hall is like a ballroom
Polka'd with dust. Strange: you learned your freedom
From your dependence, and that long beautiful boredom
Rose armed from the gradual wreck of a girlhood frolic.
Much too young to be shut up in a tower!
You said I kept too long away from you
And so men do, I think, but it's not right:
The shoots burst from the fragile trellis, all
The buds in wild profusion lean in the air,
Crossed, straggling, heavy, burdened down.
All of us bear our load, but the free spirit
Never forgives the bondage of its peers.
We have no time, alas, for heroes now:
Beneath snug tailoring its fiery hair
And plated muscles of a Fuseli angel
Strain to express a quiddity. And you,
Your head full of such antique pictures. My fault.
I should have taken greater care of you.
You and your perfect body were my text
And all its cruces hidden. Now it's too late.
A life of caring for the insights of
Another man! I sometimes felt, with Pope
And the finest of the early editors,
That the real task lay not in tidying-up
Errors and riddles of the leaden case
But in the niceties of taste and skill,
The signposts to the choicest passages,
Reader to reader. Likewise the pleasure lay
In the approval not the scorn of moves,
And I could well have wished a silent mark
Of exclamation to adorn the Swan
Many and many a time. What can one say?
When I approved, you glowed, or seemed to glow.
Perhaps unspoken pleasure in your graces
Seemed like a deafness where in truth it was
A simple echo of your quietness.

I was there. I heard. And in the end I lost.
	At least I have preserved ascendancy
In the science. Anderssen is broken and
They tell me Morphy's mad now: shouts in the street
And follows no profession. Sues his brother
For the father's fortune. Certainly won't play chess.
Well, well. One might have guessed it, but the cause
Is none too clear. What was the truth of the matter?
Did some kind tutelary spirit lean
From the rococo clouds with ready crown,
Strike Harrwitz down and give him Anderssen,
Whose play afforded shocking evidence
Of being no longer the victor's of '51?
Did we resent his luck and nerve? For my part
I had no particular feelings, retired as I was
From practical chess. How could I risk the stakes
So rashly offered by my generous friends?
I might have played a game or two, *sans façon*.
I even steeled myself to Birmingham
And entered with a show of chivalry:
Morphy refused to play! There one has it.
The tender bloom, forced under glass, must wilt
On contact with the ordinary air.
That *you* would understand, I think, my dear!
Who gave me at the time one long cool stare.
Yet those who would perform *kotoo* before the boy
(And rush to do the same before whoever's
The times' top-sawyer) can't be satisfied
To give him endless *kudos* among themselves
Without the blowing of a penny-trumpet
To call to homage all the sentient world!
Grant the achievement, and the wish to play
David to Europe's grave Goliaths, yet
It was not such a salient episode.
There was a basic failure of the will,
A trust to risk, exploiting combinations.
Eight blindfold games, remembering all the moves?
A piece of rhetoric, the science served
To better purpose by my little handbook,
Bilguer and der Laza much improved,
And read in clubs and cafés everywhere.
	I still have that, and much besides. Or do I?

At night, after some bruxist escapade,
Waking in sweat, I pad down to this study
And stare at the piled desk and all these papers
To which the attached ink is a history
Of a long hunger and fatal miscalculation.
I could be Claudius at prayer! But no,
That's silly. Even a villain has some presence.
Once proud of my pride in what I had achieved,
Now I have only the abject achievement.
Once in love with the harmony of our orbits,
Now I feel only the fierce lack at the centre.
I've risked nothing and everything is lost!
Ah, well. The deadly promptness of the spring
Becomes a kind of welcome remedy.
Its scenery is sufficient. It obeys
The rules. Those ducks, the ostentatious roses,
Even the diligent editor of Shakespeare,
All move in free compulsion to one end
Which though unknown is wholly necessary
And has some joys, I think. Or sometimes does.

THE ILLUSIONISTS

Chapter Six
The Breakfast

> she gallops night by night
> Through lovers' brains, and then they dream of love.
>   *Shakespeare*

(Tim works at Art Treasures International for the crooked
dealer Distimuth, who is in the process of selling an elaborate
fake to a Lebanese buyer. Tim and his colleague Nico are
competing for the favours of a notorious and elusive beauty
called Polly Passenger. Tim has barely noticed the ATI secretary
Mary, who herself suffers the attentions of Distimuth. In this
extract Mary dreams about Tim.)

1

Naked is how we come and naked
Is how we dance back to that world
Whose sense is only what we make it
When the still body, tightly curled
In rooted embryonic panic,
Lies like a hostage to titanic
Oblivion-demanding night
While all our spirits carry light
And reason to a strange created
Inner stage where actions are
Disordered, all phenomena
Overdifferentiated
And everything taken to extremes:
I mean, of course, the world of dreams.

2

Where now we find the sleeping Mary,
Her profile on the pillow in
Her childhood bed (a solitary
Bottom bunk in origin,
Now somewhat prettified: the other
Was slept in by her younger brother
Two rooms away) and her still brain
Alive in its occult terrain
Where passions act without rehearsal
And the strict will in full control
Tells the mind's cameras to roll
On scenes whose lure is universal
Though they were never looked upon
Save by an audience of one.

3

What did she see? An endless mirror
With figures passing in and out
Of it, and so becoming clearer.
At first each visage was in doubt
And might have been her own, reflected,
But when the melting glass bisected
The blurred insignia of the face
It put the figure in its place
And gave a name to it. On meeting
Within her dream each mirror-shape
Making reflection its escape
She moved her lips in silent greeting,
But naturally no one heard.
The figures passed without a word.

4

The first was corpulent and sinister,
Wearing his eyebrows like a threat:
Walter Retlaw, Tory minister
Who put the country into debt
By pushing with patrician bonhomie
A cut-throat system of economy.

With him was Samuel Leumas who
Appeared a deeper shade of blue
If that were possible, his features
Contracted to a line of pain
Subtended by a weary brain
That also drafted Retlaw's speeches
Where eloquence and hatred joined
In every slogan that he coined.

5

The two were followed by that solemnest
Of jesters, Graham Maharg, who played
The easy game of being a columnist
Of whom his readers were afraid:
In bed-sits, semis, mews and manses
They cowered at his fads and fancies.
From his front pocket peeped the fine
Orectic bust of Enid Dine,
Her coiffure shiny as a Sheaffer,
Her mouth agape as with the need
To say extempore the Creed
Or take, with grace, a Popish wafer.
Instead, she could be heard to sing
Better-known highlights from *The Ring*.

6

Then from another (left-hand) pocket
Glared Sir Ron Norris, union boss,
Nostrils like an electric socket
(Though hairy) arguing the toss
At annual negotiations
About industrial relations.
Graham Maharg knew when and where
To animate this puppet-pair.
If short of copy (and even more so
During a national alarm
When comedy could do no harm)
He slipped a hand into each torso
To praise or scorn speech or introit
At festive Blackpool or Bayreuth.

7

The mirror yielded further figures:
Escaped industrialist Mark Kram,
The teeth of Eric Cire, the sniggers
Of Sidney Yendis, the pure ham
Of Noël Leon, arch and cosy
Much-travelled Ysobel le Bosy,
Robert Trebor doing time
For little kidnapped Emily Lime,
Lord Droll holding a lighted taper
Beneath his nanny for a joke,
And many more. When Mary woke
She found she'd dreamed the morning paper
Where all put in a daily stint
And acted out their lives in print.

8

But still the night was not quite over
And there was one more face to dream.
Like love eluding Casanova,
A radio star, *Enigma*'s theme,
Its actual lineaments were traceless
And in her dream this face was faceless.
The kiss was casual and direct,
Surprising, chaste and circumspect,
Imbued with sadness not surrender
Like the full moon above a hill
That must in time be gone, and will
Perhaps not come again, a tender
Contact and its brief eclipse:
A silencing finger on the lips.

9

At which she really woke, a mystery
To her, but not to you, I think,
Who have been following this history
By scanning rows of signs in ink:
The things which tend to make us tenser
Are often struck out by our Censor
Who leaves it to the guilty Id
To hoard the facts it would forbid.

Were you or I to know who kisses
Us in dreams, who chases us
And whom we chase, voluptuous,
Along the edge of precipices,
We might improve our self-esteem
But then, there'd be no need to dream.

10

At breakfast all the world lay folded
In black and white against the milk.
Singers sulked and generals scolded
(Those in khaki, these in silk),
Some crooks were jailed for wielding axes
And others for avoiding taxes
While others still were knighted for
Their murdering or avoiding more.
Life thus proclaimed itself, profusely,
To Fairlea Crescent, Number 4,
Where, single and awake once more,
Mary sat down and ate her muesli:
Toothpaste and cereal combined
To put the kissing out of mind.

11

'Mary, *have* an egg,' her mother
Pleaded. 'Look, there's one just done.'
John said: 'I wouldn't mind another.
I can't keep up my strength on one.'
Every family's breakfast chatter
Is much the same: it doesn't matter,
And working girls have other things,
From hard facts to imaginings,
To think about. Her present worry,
Her cross, dead loss and albatross,
Involved attention from her boss:
'Sorry, Mum, I've got to hurry.
Mr Distimuth said he
Would very kindly call for me.'

12

'Hallo, hallo,' said John. 'What's cooking?
Lifts to the office in his car?
Pity he isn't better-looking,
Or aren't you so particular?'
'John, that's enough,' his mother chided.
'Finish your toast. Your tie's lop-sided.
And look: it's nearly ten past eight.
Get on with it or you'll be late.'
Being a widow in East Pinner
She didn't mention Distimuth,
Fearing that something was afoot
Beginning with lifts, moving to dinner
And after-dinner mints and verse
And after-dinner-something-worse.

13

And Mary thought so too. They neither
Spoke but moved about the sink
In silent contemplation, either
Washing or drying. What we think
We never speak; in conversation
We never think — dismal equation!
She took the paper to the loo
To do there what she had to do,
And found, somewhere between the Sporting
And City page, a photograph
Clearly designed to make you laugh,
A gem of straight-faced news reporting
Which showed that Polly Passenger
Had danced with a new follower.

14

Tim's name, of course, was printed slightly
Wrong. The camera caught him on
The hop, grinning, with an unsightly
Lick of hair. His forehead shone.
His posture was, to put it mildly,
Ape-like: bent knees with one arm wildly
Flung, performing the latest dance
With unconcerned extravagance.

(What it was called, I've no idea.
You may supply the name yourself:
'The Hump', 'The Limp', 'The Curious Elf',
'The Trots', 'The New Orleans Brassière',
'The Dalglish Skip', 'The Eiderdown',
'The Standing-Still', 'The Lord George-Brown'.)

15

But what the photograph omitted
From its trimmed margins was the glum
And static shape of the outwitted
Nico, still of course Tim's chum
But also now his deadly rival,
Painfully struggling for survival.
He'd had his moments of success,
Acquired that girl's West End address,
Hovered about, and at one juncture
Stepped forward with strange readiness
(When on the kerb in mild distress
She stood before her Fiat's puncture)
To pump the tyre *he* had collapsed
(After some minutes had elapsed).

16

That failed to get him in the paper
(Which didn't matter all that much)
Nor in her bed (which did). Each caper
Betrayed a faulty sense of touch
In dealing with love's paraphernalia.
Nico was half in love with failure
While Tim was twice in love with what?
With youth? with love? but surely not
With Polly Passenger, a person
He could be hardly said to know,
Always half-drunk, the lights too low.
(Remember, when relations worsen,
The friend you are unfriendly with
May not be actual, but a myth).

17

And Mary's view of Tim, how valid
The Camford graduate grotesque?
Would the reality have tallied
With what she saw across her desk?
The vowels, the smile, the stoop, the shyness,
The knowledge of Plato and Aquinas,
The curious hat bought in Torquay,
Quotations from French poetry:
All these, and more, were blossoms grounded
In roots of personality
Already difficult to see
In nature's soil, so how well-founded
Could be the feelings which required
His playing satyr to her naiad?

18

Feelings which in her dream produced
That soft inevitable kiss
Anonymous and unrestricted
Upon the lips' parenthesis?
For Tim had shown no inclination
To any sort of conversation
(Still less to play it by the book
And start with the old-fashioned look
That shows with tact the way you're leading).
He didn't tease like Nico nor
Was he, like Distimuth, a bore.
It must have been the boy's good breeding
That kept him distant and polite,
Yet he could dance, it seemed, all night!

19

And here was Distimuth already
Sounding a fanfare from the street.
She grabbed a scarf, feeling unsteady
Upon her (help, still shoeless!) feet.

'Bye, Mum! Bye, John!' she called out, slipping
Into her green suède brogues and zipping
Her matching green suède shoulder bag
Stitched in dark umber zig by zag
(The bag contained a key, a diary,
Some bijou tampons for the curse,
A tube of mints, a comb, a purse,
A letter warning of the expiry
Of library tickets, a Penguin Jeeves,
Lipstick, and paper handkerchiefs).

20

Lashing a girl to bogus leather
Inside pressed steel provides a good
Excuse to be alone together
Since giving lifts, it's understood,
Is kindly meant. Some such idea
Was Distimuth's while changing gear,
Clutching and moving Mary's knee
Gently and absentmindedly
Down into top, thereby revealing
Much more of it than anyone
At ATI had ever begun
To see (though once when she'd been kneeling
With proofs of some new catalogue,
Fredge had peeped in, his eyes agog).

21

'Today, my dear, I lunch a client
Who's of great consequence to us,
In Middle-Eastern oil, a giant
Among collectors. Make a fuss
Of this one, won't you? Do it discreetly.
I trust your savoir-faire completely.
I'm having a bit of lunch sent in,
Braised carp and duckling from Tientsin,
Snow peas and noodles, and a bonus
Of baby crab. We'll drink champagne,
Or maybe Corton Charlemagne.
There's still some left. The best coronas
Of course, and coffee as only you
Can make it. That should see us through.'

22

Lifting eight fingers from the steering
Wheel in unctuous emphasis,
He smiled one of those unendearing
Smiles that require paralysis
Of upper cheek and jaw and narrowing
Of lips: the whole effect was harrowing.
His gaze, intent upon the road
In steely concentration, showed
No kindness, warmth or even pleasure
In the said luncheon he'd rehearsed,
Though as he drove and they conversed,
His hand descended at its leisure,
Patronising, plump, inert
To smoothe the folds in Mary's skirt.

23

Ugh, I can't bear it! Do let's leave them.
Mary can handle him, I'm sure.
As for these lines, it's hard to weave them
Around a scene that's so impure.
I need, in this extravaganza,
Occasionally to give my stanza
A little rest, to let it breathe,
Especially when emotions seethe
Without some corresponding action.
The car was hot, the journey long.
I see no reason to prolong
Her torture for your satisfaction.
You know what Distimuth intends.
His client waits. The chapter ends.

NOCTURNES

1

The fingers press
And they release
The hopes which else
Would stifle us.

Such brief soundings
Are like endings
Not beginnings:
Hopes are dead things.

2

Let us, as the sun grazes
The hedge, renounce the prospect
Of new happiness.

Even the tawdry relics
Of our own past hopes
Are lost for ever.

All that certitude of novelty,
That determination to do without
The timid and the shoddy.

The portraits are of interest
To no one. They are indeed
Like ourselves.

3

Admitting that it is one of the
Minor though loved surfaces of my
Brief days as a nomad of matter
(One dear body and the cloudy blue
Sphere itself come to mind as greater)

I sit above it with fingers spread
As if to heal the straitened world of
Elephant and forest which offer
Their wounded sounds into the smiling air.

4

The room is giving the fire its attention
And the fire is self-absorbed:
A studied Brahmsian *nobilmente*
Of knots and boles and bark,
Textures too fine to lose, although
The burning must continue.

Flower, stone, pomander:
The light and warmth are wasted
For the room is empty.

5

Low moments are like slow movements
where joy succeeds, *presto possibile*.

Succeeding is not success, to be sure,
Merely a dialectic of structure.

The natural ebullience of an ending
When we sense, with relief, that ending is final.

SONATA

The body leaning slightly back, the arms held firm and straight
As if she found those first deliberate chords a heavy weight
Impelling sound to herald, like the raising of a curtain,
A massive concentration on the things we find uncertain,
And with a noble carelessness of what she there might find,
She starts upon her journey to the centre of the mind.

At first the notes are confident of all they understand,
As if the sum of human purpose lies beneath each hand.
The cadences of concord cross the measured page in pairs
As calmly as a couple might descend the morning stairs
Or children playing in a garden weave the air with thirds
As though for simple happiness their calls were those of birds.

But then her eyes perceive ahead a shift in the notation.
An *allargando* of regret, bereavement's modulation,
Reveals the theme's distinction to be that of comprehending
How every ravishment contains the sourness of pretending
That in our perfect virtue it may chance to last for ever,
If destiny so smiles upon our singular endeavour.

Its falling minims lucidly declare the fight will fail
To win ourselves the closure of the lucky fairy-tale.
The sober music now decides the battle has been done.
Its message to the pianist is that nothing has been won.
Not even sheer persistence in the struggle for expression
Ever deprives the darkness of the fullness of possession.

Descending octaves falter as the left hand turns the page
Revealing flocks of quavers beating wings against their cage.
The fingers fumble wildly in their effort to release
The soul that mocks their movements from the prison of the
    piece.
She offers it the freedom that its dumbness cannot learn
Though she bargains for its ransom, trying all the keys in turn.

The music turns to panic only stubbornness denies,
As if the fingers' questions forced the vagueness of replies,
Until with all the righteousness of having come so far
It thunders to exhaustion at the final double bar.
Her hands remain a moment on the flat and silent keys
And then she slowly places them together on her knees.

128

Her head is motionless and bowed, hair faintly disarranged.
The silence holds suspended everything her hands have
    changed,
In muted echoes from the mind of what the air has lost.
Her feet have quietly drawn back from the pedals, ankles
    crossed,
As if conclusion could admonish how the sound behaves
When granted independence from the locked and blackened
    staves.

This moment is what you or I, had we been there to hear,
Would call the grave illusion of the will to persevere,
Since all except our love for her has vanished like a vapour
And nothing is at rest, or certain, save the printed paper,
For love demands a truth the music has denied in vain
And what it said contented us, and will content again.

DOZING

How much longer must I sit here
Waiting for something to happen?
The clatter of the exciting parcel
Is only the cat nosing through her door
In search of the relief her hardening kidneys
Refuse, the back leg drawn slowly through the flap
Extended behind her like a ballerina's
Who turns and turns, without a thought,
Through the repeated afternoons.

She dozes on the arms of the high fender, twitching,
Throat flattened trustingly on the padded cloth,
Tail drooping, body slipping sideways,
Till only her claws, which experience has anchored
To the warm raft of her dreams, sustain her,
And she is left hanging on like Norman Lloyd
In Hitchcock's *Saboteur*. As she climbs back
Her look is hurt, sleepy, resigned,
Like an arrested drunkard.

If I encourage her to lie on my knee
I will never move again! The bottle is out of reach,
The finishing cadences motionless on the turntable,
The amplifier's hum expectantly filling the room.
It is a moment for some truth to occur to me,
About chance, about hope, about stubbornness,
About how we are to face the unfaceable.
Notions I reckon too solemn for silence,
Too gravelling for tenderness.

TRIO

A gardener's triumph! But it was planted at an angle
And has to be supported on its frail root.
Her hands run up and down its trunk like squirrels
And she loves it like a child between her knees.

A feat of balance! But it all takes place
Between tight-rope fingers and clown-mouth
On a journey in a wooden boat with a single oar
Occurring in the guarded space belonging to kisses.

A banquet for one! But he toys with his food,
Eyes closed, head tilted back in rapture
At the enormous table, the black table,
The table with three legs and a lid.

SYRINX

Most surgical of instruments!
Aeolian tube with rods and keys
Poised in the balanced hands to squeeze
The slender soul through its precise space,
Like a rare serpent of the desert south
Worshipped in its narrow place,
Drawing the soul from the hovering mouth!

A trickle that defies gravity, creating
Pools of articulated notes that fly
From each prestidigitating hand,
A shining elevated wand
Whose buttons the fingers do up so quickly!

It is like a telescope for the wind's song
Extended from the lips and tongue
As from an eye to which horizons are strangely near.
Then the silver body is broken in three
And the music survives in the ear.

CONCERTO FOR DOUBLE BASS

He is a drunk leaning companionably
Around a lamp post or doing up
With intermittent concentration
Another drunk's coat.

He is a polite but devoted Valentino,
Cheek to cheek, forgetting the next step.
He is feeling the pulse of the fat lady
Or cutting her in half.

But close your eyes and it is sunset
At the edge of the world. It is the language
Of dolphins, the growth of tree-roots,
The heart-beat slowing down.

SILENCE

Once again the instruments
Rehearse their elaborate departure
And the eyes continue to stare ahead
When all excuse for pensiveness
Is gone, the record long unwound;
Only the miles-off surf of the speakers
Establishing its vacant musty
Presence: not worth listening to.

LILY AND VIOLIN

1

You buried them so lightly,
These crinkly globes and packages,
It seems a thought would wake them.

Slumbering in their soily shallows,
Folded waxen music of earth
That stirs like a waking shape.

The shape thinks them, breeds them,
As ink is splashed in crotchets
Across a furious page.

The instruments begin to sound.
Their warmth is the slow warmth
Of defined space, of paysage.

And the black and white of a late snow
Melts into laughter like small touching,
The giant's coloured beard.

2

A needle of lightning strikes
The black imaginary valley
As a tyro lily with inch of violet nib
Tries to scribble a message
As still as abandoned smoke
Soon to become the frail green
Of a grandmother's silk girlhood
Whirling and twisting in the snapped air.

And she encounters Herr Violin
Hiding tears beneath nobility,
The frayed sleeves of a maitre d'hotel,
Dripping traces of hot sugar
To cool in a bowl of clearest water
To thunderous applause.

3

Prue, your bulbs are out a-walking
Quite without our knowing it:
The great lighthouse lily on its stalk,
Wing-cases askew, ready to fly;
The common hyacinths in waterproof shoes,
Green shawls and paper haircurlers;
The lily-of-the-valley standing still
In a sculptured fairy cluster.

Their earth, their pebbled bowls
Yield a fragrance like a great wine.
What do they think of this world with corners
They have so achingly woken up to?
Full of dry warm air, tobacco smoke
And the sound of the sublime КВИНТЕТ?

4

The violin's voyage through the still room
Establishes a momentary map
Of things distinguished and responsive to
Its movement: books silent and tight as slate,
An empty chair, a battle-row of pawns,
The glass monstrance of a forgotten claret,
And in a corner, stretching to be away,
The six soundless sails of a great white lily.

Strangely I wish, I wish I were not here,
For only the mind among them recognises
(How unwilling, how ungenerous!)
The vain deception of its call to action,
The wildness of its promises, how soon
It will all end, the deadness of the dead.

5

Here we are, then, half in and half out
Of what, being in such a position,
It is almost impossible to describe
Except in terms of the small events
Which shadow its embracing dimension
And please us by seeming to be other than it.

Like the sustained rich impure
Voluntary of the stroked string
Doubling itself and redoubling,
In motion still, although the sound
No longer reaches the ear. So that
We almost hope to be wrong in saying
With Duke Mantee that we expect
To spend the rest of our lives dead.

6

Afterwards we may not speak: piled chords
Are broken open with changes of key;
Logs in settling shoot a surprising flame;
A petal folds more slowly than night falls;
A face is lifted to catch the last
Ache of struggling body or air.

Afterwards we may not speak, since
Everything hastens towards its end
With an enlarging beauty. May not,
Need not, will not, we say, obsessed
Like vagrant creatures with consummation.
But it is all our dear illusion
Belonging to the experience itself
Which must not speak of afterwards.

7

I was reading of Samuel and Sara's cottage
With its talismans of jasmine and myrtle
Preserved in splashes of exclamations
When I saw you carrying away the bowls
Of lilies like the toyed leavings
Of a pampered flower-eating god!

Dead, are they? Dry already?
And was there nothing to preserve them
Except those simple marks shared
Across almost two hundred years
With the dreaming poet whose
Utopia was a failed commune,
His Arcadia an accessible breast?
It is you, Prue, my eyes follow, not lilies.

After their brief incarnation
The bulbs are returned to the garden
And the room is without life.

Sounds have now no shapes to charm
Beyond this clutter whose collapse
Extends beyond a year.

The spring was counterfeit
Like the excited emotions
Of our own first flowering.

Before experiment was experience,
Before discovery was recognition,
Before the event became activity.

And we are left now with our patience,
The sleeping of beauty unaroused,
The silence between the movements.

WAITING FOR THE MUSIC

This is the news: two sounds
At a guarded melodious distance
Follow each other wherever
Either chooses to go.

And all our lives we are
Waiting for the music,
Waiting, waiting for the music.

Scanning the instructions,
Hand reaching for hand.

Waiting for the music.

RETREAT

I should like to live in a sunny town like this
Where every afternoon is half-day closing
And I would wait at the terminal for the one train
Of the day, pacing the platform, and no one arriving.

At the far end of the platform is a tunnel, and the train
Slows out of it like a tear from a single eye.
You couldn't get further than this, the doors all opened
And the porter with rolled sleeves wielding a mop.

Even if one restless traveller were to arrive
With leather grip, racquets under the arm,
A belted raincoat folded over the shoulder,
A fishing hat, and a pipe stuck in his mouth,

There would be nowhere for him to move on to
And he would settle down to tea in the lounge
Of the Goat Hotel, doing yesterday's crossword,
And would emerge later, after a nap, for a drink.

You meet them in the bar, glassy-eyed, all the time.
They never quite unpack, and expect letters
From one particular friend who doesn't write.
If you buy them a drink they will tell you their life history:

'I should have liked to live in a sunny town like this,
Strolling down to the harbour in the early evening,
Looking at the catch. Nothing happens here.
You could forget the ill-luck dogging you.

'I could join the Fancy Rat Society and train
Sweet peas over the trellised porch
Of my little slice of stuccoed terrace. I could
Be in time for the morning service at Tesco's.

'I expect death's like this, letters never arriving
And the last remembered failure at once abandoned
And insistent, like a card on a mantelpiece.
What might it be? You can take your choice.

' "I shook her by the shoulders in a rage of frustration."
"I smiled, and left the room without saying a word."
"I was afraid to touch her, and never explained."
"I touched her once, and that was my greatest mistake." '

You meet them before dinner. You meet them after dinner,
The unbelieved, the uncaressed, the terrified.
Their conversation is perfectly decent but usually
It slows to a halt and they start to stare into space.

You would like it here. Life is quite ordinary
And the self-pity oozes into the glass like bitters.
What's your poison? Do you have a desire to drown?
We're all in the same boat. Join us. Feel free.

And when the bar closes we can say good-bye
And make our way to the terminal where the last
(Or is it the first?) train of the day is clean and waiting
To take us slowly back to where we came from.

But will we ever return? Who needs us now?
It's the town that requires us, though the streets are empty.
It's become a habit and a retreat. Or a form of justice.
Living in a sunny town like this.

TOPKAPI

I am the sultan. Jewelled, I sit on jewels.
My head bows with the weight of jewels.
My fingers curl open with the weight of jewels.

They bring me a bowl of emeralds the size of figs
To play with if I want to, and curds
To eat with spoons so diamonded
They rasp my lower lip.

I have a candlestick
With 6666 diamonds. The British Queen
Has sent me the jewelled order of her garter.

One day I will throw myself into the Bosphorus.

SULTAN AHMET SQUARE

In Sultan Ahmet Square
The brass domes of the pots
In the boot-boy's box
Echo the domes of the mosque
On which one seems to step
As if to threaten Blefuscu
While on the leather are mixed
The browns and blues and blacks
That would let a Whistler daub
A dissimilar sky to the sky
From which now Allah leans
To admire his shining toe-caps.

FUATPAŞA CADDESI

On Fuatpaşa Caddesi
A man stands all day in the mud
With ten bedsteads against a railing.
They are for sale, but no one buys.

Down Çadircilar Caddesi
A man staggers as though inspecting the mud
With ten mattresses roped to his back.
He is taking them somewhere from somewhere else.

In the evening they drink warm salep by the bridge
And the cinnamon tickles their throats!

GALATA BRIDGE

They stand patiently in doorways
Fingering their rifles like exhibitionists.
Eyes are averted from bayonets.
Crowds pass busily, resigned like brides.

They are required to look serious in case
Anyone pauses long enough to laugh,
And because their upper lips are shaven,
Leaving them vulnerable and naked.

There is a tank by the Galata Bridge
Which has not come down the steep streets
Nor over the bridge, which rocks in frail sections
That let through the dawn shipping.

It is positioned here mysteriously
Angled on its concrete eminence,
As though by a boy kneeling with a toy,
Breathing heavily, placing it exactly.

MOSQUE

One hand keeps a scarf to the mouth, the other
Holds the paired shoes lightly at waist level
Like the violinist's finished flourish of the bow,
The eyes looking down in modesty and concentration.

Carpets layer the stone, careless, unstinting.
A patch of window shows rain, and a ship passing.
The dome muffles whispers like a yawn, and on
The grandfather clock are numerals like closed umbrellas.

Outside, the rituals of trade and government
Continue to gather and disperse the organisms
Which here have no place in the everlasting designs.
That weave their studied intervals around you.

Except for a few flowers you may warily tread on
As you walk further and further into the silence
Or find repeated in the baked gardens of the walls
That reach their blue and orange to the dome.

PRAYER

Prayer is talking to these beautiful inventions
And is agreed to be a performance
Best conducted in a professional silence.

Beneath the great hanging circles of lamps
On the rich carpets they settle themselves
And begin to practise their headstands.

Don't we recognise the pretence
From our own feinted applause?

ST SOPHIA

Two figures there beneath the dome, walking with similar pace,
Turned as the other turned, forward and back, in that empty
   space.

Turning on the heel, looking about, casual but intense,
With everything that might belong to a stranger's cautious
   grace.

Eyes like hands went out to the marble and stone and precise
   gold
On the walls where the guarding images left a broken trace.

In the narthex, in the galleries, in the side-aisles,
Up and down, as drawn to each other as to that echoing place.

As though it were the whole world, and I saw the man was
   myself
And he walked there with the woman and the woman had your
   face.

ÇİÇEK PASAJI

Here on the dirty edge of everything
The streets are dark, pleasure uncertain.
But the fish and flowers are bright
As the loud throats of the stallkeepers!

Pipes of bones, and wigs and shawls of tripes;
Fish like wet embryos of fallen angels
Head down or gills unhinged
Caught by a beneficent fisherman
At some willed apocalyptic abortion
Of all the other world; lights behind glass;
Tulips on fire; spices bright as pigments;
Hissing of cooking; globes of oranges;
Our tight fingers, interlaced in wool.

And in dark alleys, a flickering bucket,
The hopeful outcast's fire.

IRONING

1 *Handkerchiefs*

They are impressed, imposed in 16mo
And lastly collated, the fingers walking up
Their ladder of warm cotton corners like money.

Later, when they are needed, they are carefully opened
And stared at, as though counterfeit, in the frozen
Instantaneous disbelief of a sneeze.

2 *Jeans*

The board is hard between their legs
As they cling in abject fear of being
Thrown. Endurance is an ignominy,
Branded on the bum by a gothic arch.

3 *Shirts*

Collars crease into smiles, the weak armpits
Are tickled and the empty wrists hang limply.
The heat relaxes and the stroking appeases
The possible flap and flutter of spooky sleeves.

There are mornings when we bound upstairs
And open their coffins simply to establish
That they are still lying in peaceable folds
Under pungent sachets of prophylactic herbs.

How may we exorcize them? Mirrors reflect
The innocent idiot smirk of a confident victim
Careless of their guile which requires him to tighten
The fatal noose around his own neck, too.

WASP NEST

Be careful not to crush
This scalloped tenement:
Who knows what secrets
Winter has failed to find
Within its paper walls?

It is the universe
Looking entirely inwards,
A hanging lantern
Whose black light wriggles
Through innumerable chambers

Where hopes still sleep
In her furry pews,
The chewed dormitory
Of a forgotten tribe
That layered its wooden pearl.

It is a basket of memories,
A museum of dead work,
The spat Babel of summer
With a marvellous language
Of common endeavour.

Note: it is the fruit
Returning to the tree,
The world becoming a clock
For sleep, a matrix of pure
Energy, a book of many lives.

SIGNS

Talking to animals? The animal novel?
To hell with the stable ego of gorilla!
We look for signs. And she does sign,
Though with a dark air of abstractedness.
'Beans hurry give me beans.'
O lovely behaviour of silksad gorilla!
Is coal or soot, immortal coal or soot!

OLD THINGS

The nest in the sycamore has outlasted
The night's wind, but was already
Empty, its twigs just as unuseful
As these on the lawn of the morning's damage,
Its role bizarre, challenging, symbolic,
Like a crown in a bush on a battlefield.

The old barometer has traced
The wind's descent on its cylinder
Of paper, the loops of ink lapping
Its chequered weeks like a prize miler,
The information, required or not,
Accumulating under the glass.

These things stir the heart with regret
For all our fruitless struggles and hopes,
The lost chances, the hoarded rubbish.

UNCERTAINTIES

These moments of waiting
For an unarranged meeting
Are full of the strangest uncertainties
As the mind delightedly shifts in its willing vertigo.

Imagine a book deciding
Upon this or that meaning
In that close second before you open it,
The loose print tumbling together, the hand on the doorknob!

What will be, will be.
Everything has its way.
What did you expect from the encounter?
Did you think your life would be changed like the end of a
    chapter?

Decision is a failing
To understand feeling,
How it responds eagerly to the response.
Books are beautiful but dead. Who is reading whom?

Or perhaps the event's reversal
Was designed by rehearsal
And the future is simply the tide you swim with
Turning page after page after page after page after page.

THE WOOD

This wood is not a wood to hide in.
It is a place to run about in,
A place where both the shoulders show
At once and the thin trees inclining
One to the other make tangled arches
That you must brush aside as you pass.

Where you stop, six ladybirds
As it might be hibernating
In a tree's armpit. Each pair
Of wing-cases as closely folded
As the stiff glass and gold leaves
Of an old time-piece, not going.

Have you looked up and seen something
Disappearing that was not a branch
Or the quick bird that left it nodding,
Curious for buds? Something that left
The grey and violet air more conscious
Of the still space it occupied?

If you do run, the dead trees
Stirring in broken sleep beneath you,
All you do is find yourself
In a different part of the same wood.
And no one seeing you can be sure
That they have seen you. And no one is there.

PRIMROSE

With one knee arched over the ditch,
Finger and thumb reaching for the base of the stem,
I can't recall what the word was I'd forgotten.

Perhaps it was something the heart thought,
Loud in its cave of blood. If so, no matter.
I know I'll remember. Perhaps when I least want to.

For now the flower speaks in my hand.
The deep yellow at its centre melts to the petals,
A perfect wash. Its memory is in its face.

ABSENCE

What can the world worse arrange
Than its encounters in time and place?
Imagine a girl taking her horse
Towards the sun. Frowning slightly,
She pushes back the hair from her eyes.

A walker, striding with cut switch
The length of a cropped valley, the wind
Just strong enough for new lambs
To lean into, finds nothing to swing at
Except a patch of opening gorse.

When an Easter butterfly
Weaves out of it, giddy with hope,
His gloom is complete. There on the sward
Are clustered the shallow clear mud-ghosts
Of horseshoes. Which might be hers. But aren't.

AMAZING

So many numbered tracts,
So many pictured acts
And unexpected facts
    Saw I never;
So many bedroom arts,
So many private parts
And so few affected hearts
    Saw I never.

Such hiding and showing,
Such coming and going,
Such ahing and ohing
    Saw I never;
So many jobs for the hands
And explored hinterlands,
So many well-used glands
    Saw I never.

So many genuflections
Before soft erections,
So many false affections
    Saw I never;
So much thrashing and snorting,
So much fruitless exhorting
And such sad consorting
    Saw I never.

So little forbidden
To the bedridden,
So little hidden
    Saw I never;
So many immersions
In corrupt versions,
Such cheap excursions
    Saw I never.

Such drooping and dragging,
Such feinting and flagging,
Such sighing and sagging
    Saw I never;

So many waves and handstands
At cheering grandstands
And thumping bandstands
     Saw I never.

So many hopeless triers,
So many falsifiers,
So many downright liars
     Saw I never;
Such long thrasonical
And unironical
Erotic chronicle
     Saw I never.

So many greetings
And frequent meetings,
Such silent entreatings
     Saw I never.
So many on the brink
Of the fourth or fifth drink
Wasting their love in ink
     Saw I never.

WORDS

Tongue is surface, too, though hidden.
Talking is an act, though hated.
Hands are still that would be moving
Over and over, but in silence.

Words are meeting, perhaps, though mistaken.
Lips are doorways, though on chains.
Heads are tilted, as before kissing
Over and over, but in silence.

Touch is withheld, often, though wanted.
Language claims lives, though wasted.
Eyes do much that the body would do
Over and over, but in silence.

LINDA

1

Linda, Linda, slender and pretty,
Biscuit girl in a biscuit city,
Packing the biscuits in paper boxes,
What do you dream of? How do you dream?
The cutters rise and fall and rise and cut
The chocolate, the coconut,
The Orange Princess and the Gypsy Cream.
The biscuits gather and the boxes shut,
But things are never what they seem.

In the school the bells are ringing,
In the playground girls are singing:
  Lily, paper, hard-boiled eggs,
  Mr Swain has bandy legs.
Linda, Linda, rude and sweet,
Skipping girl in a skipping street,
Singing and skipping all summer long:
  Worms in the classroom, worms in the hall,
  Mr Swain will eat them all.

The cutters fall and rise and fall
And biscuits are unending like a wall
And school is over and the summer's dream.

2

The day the sun invented flowers again
Her heart unfolded with the spring.
Paul had appeared and nothing was the same.

  The railway's on its sleepers,
  The river's in its bed,
  All Berkshire is beneath us and
  The sky is overhead.

Linda crossed the platform to the train.
Her warm little mouth reached up to his
And kissed and whispered his exciting name.

What was it like before we met?
What did we ever do?
Can't think of anything like it
Or anyone like you.

Weaving fingers find out that they fit
And all the secret pleasures they commit
Are like the touch of flowers in the rain.

3

A whistle from the primus:
The water's nice and hot.
I've got the milk and sugar
And teabags in the pot.
Sometimes there are sandwiches
And sometimes there are not,
But fishing is a fiddle
And Paul requires his tea.
He hasn't time to make it
So he leaves it all to me,
And there are always biscuits
(I bring along the tin.
I think it might be useful
To put the fishes in).
Fishing on the island, only me and him,
Fishing on the island all the afternoon,
The river flowing by us, full to the brim,
And the fishing is over all too soon.

When I packed the basket
Was there something I forgot?
It says *Plum* on the label
And Paul likes apricot.
I usually forget things
Though sometimes I do not,
But fishing is a fiddle
And Paul requires his tea.
He hasn't time to make it
So he leaves it all to me,
And there are always biscuits
(I bring along the tin.
I think it might be useful
To put the fishes in).

Fishing on the island, only me and him,
Fishing on the island all the afternoon,
The river flowing by us, full to the brim,
And the fishing is over all too soon.

The river's full of fishes.
You'd think he'd catch a lot.
I'll call out: 'Have you got one?'
And Paul will answer: 'What?'
Sometimes he will land one
And most times he will not,
But fishing is a fiddle
And Paul requires his tea,
And when his basket's empty
He holds it out to me
And grins to say he's sorry
(I love that silly grin
And I find it very useful
To put my kisses in).
Kissing on the island, only me and him,
Kissing on the island all the afternoon,
The river flowing by us, full to the brim,
And the kissing is over all too soon.

4

When we went down to Maidenhead
Paul had his clarinet.
I tried to do the steering and
We both got very wet.
But how he blew that liquorice stick!
The music on a thread
Rose like a nest of rooks above
His black and curly head.

There's a rookery at Dorney
But all the rooks have gone,
Flapping their wings like overcoats
They're struggling to put on.
I love their wild black music,
But all the rooks have gone.

We took a tent and Mum was mad.
Paul had his clarinet.
I had this spoon and china mug:
We made a fine duet.
But how he blew that wooden throat
Like a musical millionaire!
The black night-sound inside forced out
In squiggles on the air.

There's a rookery at Dorney
But all the rooks have gone,
And clouds blow over empty trees
Where once the summer shone,
And Paul and his black music
And all his love, have gone.

5

Linda went out in her wedges.
The day was average,
And masses of water were moving
Under Caversham Bridge.

Paul had promised to meet her
And take her on the river.
She looked again at her wristwatch
And gave a little shiver.

Well, wasn't he worth forgiving?
The hour ticked slowly on,
And she threw her Wrigley paper
Down at a frowning swan.

Several boys passed by her
And all of them managed to stare.
But Linda looked right through them
As if she didn't care.

You believe him if he tells you.
You think he's ever so nice
And it's hard to find he can never
Say the same thing twice.

Promises break like biscuits.
Nothing keeps for ever.
But time runs on and on and on,
Deep as the lying river.

6

Linda, Linda, older and wiser,
Far from childhood in a biscuit town,
Making biscuits where the Thames winds down,
Under the eyes of the supervisor,
Under the hands of the factory clock:
    Tick, tick, tick, tick,
      Crisp and crumbly, thin and thick.
The cutters rise and fall and rise,
Cutting out (surprise, surprise)
The chocolate, the coconut,
The Orange Princess and the Gypsy Cream.

But things are never what they seem.
The trains pass clanking on the track,
Distinct and jewelled in the quiet night:
    Tick, tick, tick, tick,
      In life's absurd arithmetic.
And Linda in the tunnel of her dream
All night is restless, staring back
As wisps of the dragon drift into the wind
And, smaller and smaller, Paul is waving,
Smaller and smaller, Paul is standing there.
And Linda dreams and dreams and dreams
Under the hands of the bedside clock,
Till bacon smells are in the air
And combs tug sleepily through morning hair
And nothing is ever what it seems.

VALENTINE

The things about you I appreciate
    May seem indelicate:
I'd like to find you in the shower
And chase the soap for half an hour.
I'd like to have you in my power
    And see your eyes dilate.
I'd like to have your back to scour
And other parts to lubricate.
Sometimes I feel it is my fate
To chase you screaming up a tower
    Or make you cower
By asking you to differentiate
    Nietzsche from Schopenhauer.
I'd like successfully to guess your weight
    And win you at a fête.
I'd like to offer you a flower.

I like the hair upon your shoulders,
Falling like water over boulders.
I like the shoulders, too: they are essential.
Your collar-bones have great potential
(I'd like all your particulars in folders
    Marked *Confidential*).

I like your cheeks, I like your nose,
I like the way your lips disclose
The neat arrangement of your teeth
(Half above and half beneath)
    In rows.

I like your eyes, I like their fringes.
The way they focus on me gives me twinges.
Your upper arms drive me berserk.
I like the way your elbows work,
    On hinges.

I like your wrists, I like your glands,
I like the fingers on your hands.
I'd like to teach them how to count,
And certain things we might exchange,

Something familiar for something strange.
I'd like to give you just the right amount
    And get some change.

I like it when you tilt your cheek up.
I like the way you nod and hold a teacup.
I like your legs when you unwind them.
Even in trousers I don't mind them.
I like each softly-moulded kneecap.
I like the little crease behind them.
I'd always know, without a recap,
    Where to find them.

I like the sculpture of your ears.
I like the way your profile disappears
Whenever you decide to turn and face me.
I'd like to cross two hemispheres
    And have you chase me.
I'd like to smuggle you across frontiers
Or sail with you at night into Tangiers.
    I'd like you to embrace me.

I'd like to see you ironing your skirt
    And cancelling other dates.
I'd like to button up your shirt.
I like the way your chest inflates.
I'd like to soothe you when you're hurt
Or frightened senseless by invert-
    ebrates.

I'd like you even if you were malign
And had a yen for sudden homicide.
I'd let you put insecticide
    Into my wine.
I'd even like you if you were the Bride
    Of Frankenstein
Or something ghoulish out of Mamoulian's
    Jekyll and Hyde.
I'd even like you as my Julian
Of Norwich or Cathleen ni Houlihan.
    How melodramatic
If you were something muttering in attics
Like Mrs Rochester or a student of Boolean
    Mathematics.

You are the end of self-abuse.
You are the eternal feminine.
I'd like to find a good excuse
To call on you and find you in.
I'd like to put my hand beneath your chin,
 And see you grin.
I'd like to taste your Charlotte Russe,
I'd like to feel my lips upon your skin,
I'd like to make you reproduce.

I'd like you in my confidence.
I'd like to be your second look.
I'd like to let you try the French Defence
 And mate you with my rook.
I'd like to be your preference
 And hence
I'd like to be around when you unhook.
I'd like to be your only audience,
The final name in your appointment book,
 Your future tense.

GONE TO GROUND

Veuve du Vernay in the gutter, flattened wire and querns of cork
Mark where candidates vacated (like the elders of the Kirk
Joining in a witches' rout) the holy temple of their rites –
Schola Magna Borealis – spilling gowned inebriates.
Prior to every paper, files of desks were sown with writing-books
Germinating inkily beneath the working rows of backs;
Pentels played superbly in the cradles of their moving fists;
Silent whispers to the ceiling charmed the peacocks, prayed for
 Firsts;
Fingers propped up profiles Buonarroti might have liked to
 carve;
Unimaginable beauties shut in pallor like a cave
On a friendly surface flowers and antihistamines had made
Brought to life the latent heroines of *My Last Duchess*, *Maud*,
Nineteenth century victims of the poet's urge to wield his power
Over girls not fully understood, bold, self-possessed though pure
(When their knowledge faltered, Kleenex, sweets and mascots
 were employed).
Schools became a theatre where the memory and passion
 played,
Empty all the summer once the fustian black and white had
 gone
(Tennyson and Browning are allowed to lie unread again).
Down the High Street stroll unhindered naked knees and tartan
 paunch,
Cluny's closed and Honey's empty save for someone buying
 Punch.
All the mysteries enacted now are commonplace once more,
Sacred circumstances simply something travellers can admire.
Evidence is trapped unnoticed in the omnipresent lens:
Businessmen from Nagasaki freeze as one of them aligns
What remains of Magdalen Tower with an antiseptic grin,
CANDY underfoot and to the right a door of brass and green.
On the other corner Oxford Travel Agents are relieved:
Sheaves of booking stubs reveal where students' lives are now
 being lived.
Transalpino, Apex, Eurotrain and private bus convey
Heart-struck, star-crossed, shattered souls to gaze upon a
 different view.
Foreign cities heal with culture wounds that culture has
 induced,

Love forgotten as the banger jolts through fascinating dust.
Soppy sentimental disconnected drainpipes go their ways,
Finding in a summer's absence much inducement to be wise.
Term was going out to dinner, giving bear-hugs in the quad,
Heads together over just the quantity of work required.
Literature is what you make it and it's bound to turn to tears.
Now it's nature's turn to comfort as the dear ideal retires:
Thumbs along the autostrada bring an everchanging view;
Tents in Sligo echo with the savage wounding of a vow.
Human lineaments will alter since you make them what they
    seem;
Rocks and water are unyielding for their substance is the same.
Wordsworth told us once and we were almost willing to believe
(Keeping fingers crossed behind our back because we knew that
    love
Conquered after all each famous effort to be understood,
Offering the various shapes of dull eternity instead).
Passion doesn't bear examination – though perhaps it should
Shaping as it does the source from which all mental life is shed.
Ardent alpha-minus and besotted beta-plus, God knows,
Can't be much preferred to grieving gamma, narcissist NS,
Given our agreement on the joy of unrequited love,
Caring only that its fatal feelings may be kept alive,
Never to be disappointed by their hope of being fulfilled
Like a conjuror's spectators who are eager to stay fooled.
Don't expect a tutor to stay moping in a tourist town:
Bright at the receiver you will only hear the dialling tone.
If you're passing through yourself, perhaps to bring me back
    some books
(Quantities I lent you: won't you need to put them in a box?)
Don't imagine I'll be waiting, kettle steaming, on the hour.
Did you call? I'm sorry! I'm afraid that's just the way things are.
Was my room locked and the tap not dripping, friendly, on the
    stair?
Did the scout look blank and turn away and give her tea a stir?
Did you interrupt the Lodge's cricket, stamp and tear your hair?
Hearing Strutt recite his lesson: 'Mr Fuller is not here,
Having taken up a new appointment as the top masseur
(Being handy, tender, ready, when the nape and hips are sore)
With the Russian women's swimming, pole-vault and
    gymnastic teams,
Keen, you see, on sport and travel when he isn't keeping terms.
Leave a message with the porter? Always happy to oblige.

Got a packet for him, have you? Hope it isn't very large.
Look his pigeon hole is full already: invitations, cheques,
Magazines and scented envelopes as soft as ladies' cheeks.
Come back in October (what's the phrase?–"the sere and yellow
   leaf")
Michaelmas, I'm sure, will see us all resuming normal life.'
Life! Ah, life, who always lives us so intensely at his will;
Life in lying chapters, promising that things will soon be well;
Life, who understands us all but keeps the secret in his book;
Life, the truest friend – who, once he goes away, will not come
   back.

THE COLLEGE GHOST

For Hugh Sinclair

At 11.25, after a college beano
Designed to wish a retiring colleague well
(Who with a glass in one hand, a watch in the other
Like the pieces of Alice's mushroom, sat and then rose
To remind with smiling words why we shall miss him),

At that suspended hour of a summer night,
Having made my few farewells, collected my gown,
My black tie carelessly telling the approximate time,
The claret filling my toes, the toes my shoes
And the shoes knowing more or less the way to go,

I left the smoking-room and paced the cloisters
In the wrong direction, almost three sides where one
Would do, to find the passage to take me safely
To the only place where we regularly fall
Utterly unconscious without rebuke or danger

And came at once upon the college ghost
Lolling in a Gothic arch not far from the kitchens.
It had a gross nonchalant air, pretending
That it simply chanced to be there waiting for no one
Particularly, picking its non-existent nails.

Its face was puffy and indistinct, the eyes
Burnt holes, nose gone, the grin healthy
But upside down. It wore a college scarf
And a row of pens in its shroud like a boffin,
Slouched in its window in a May Week pose.

It watched me as I approached and it made its greeting,
Not deferent, not assertive, simply assuming
Its right to expect me to stop, as though our notes
Had crossed and whatever it was had there and then
To be settled and some confusion straightened out.

The night was dark and winy as a cellar,
The only noises the clacking of the flagpole
On St Swithun's tower and the thumping of my heart.
But I wasn't surprised. I felt it was an encounter
Fated at one or another time to occur.

I fingered the keys in my pocket, the inner and outer
Circuits, comforting brass and heavy for turning
The secret doors and great gates of the college,
Fingered them as though they were amulets
To keep at a distance the presence I found before me.

Behind and through it gleamed the broad green square
Of the lawn where all that summer afternoon
In various attitudes of conversation
Undergraduates had sat with early teas
Outlapping the lingering remains of lunch

And the voice of the shapeless shape, if voice it was,
Drifted towards me softly, catching my ear
Exactly like a carefully-placed loudspeaker,
And its words were the words of all who had sat on that lawn
Through similar afternoons until such darkness fell:

'Though I am not often seen here, at least at times
When troublesome tasks last through daylight or take
You from page to page of assorted memoranda,
Nose down like a broker or a winded traveller
Frantic for the last train in a foreign city,

'Though I am discrepant and uncorroborated
As a reputation; embarrassing as the memory
Of insufficient words at parting; feared
Like a summons for a forgotten misdemeanour;
Still, I do appear, and appear to you now.

'It's precisely at times like this, when you are distracted
By well-being and owl-light from shutting your senses
To what I represent and am ready to communicate
That I eagerly seize my chance to materialise
Like an image on paper in a paddled tray.

'You reckon you can shortly make your escape,
Say more next time. So be it. That is your manner.
But for the moment, stay. I have something to tell you
That has been keeping but will not keep for ever,
Like Clipsham stone or a Pomerol, but not so nice.

'It concerns the conspiracy to keep me partly asleep
With promise of distinct pleasures belonging to
The forms of success towards which you propelled me,
Wise like an elder framing a constitution
Before he retires and dies a powerless legend.

'You gave me much that could not shame the giver
Whatever whoops of joy and sounds of breakage
Greeted your smiles, fond as a distant uncle,
When the package was ripped open, the contents spilled,
The crucial instructions immediately lost.

'But grammar burned bishops and nations fell to the prism.
I negotiated the quantities of blood required
To put into effect the decrees of the Ineffable.
I argued over heads that I knew were soon
To lose all interest in what they commandeered.

'I was present when the planet first took its header
Into the bracing briny of the impermanent.
I dignified the scribbled with the spacing of nuts and muttons.
I bowed in Washington, once the place was invented.
Through me the Greeks discovered Australia.

'Theories of diet dispersed tribes, infections
Accompanied stately truths like interpreters.
I took your towers for wit, your lawns for sorrow,
And made the friendships that reduced brown acres
Of imposing mahogany to the space of a handclasp.

'Even when the world in a more appealing tongue
Spoke of the price to be paid for a share of power,
It was to you I referred with a slight shrug
And perhaps a mock self-deprecatory grin
That could not decide if it cared for your approval.

174

'You gave it. And that was when I became a ghost,
Rioting invisibly in the halls and staircases
Of my consecrated youth, while everything true
And good fell from my fingers or from windows,
Drifting like laughter in the direction of the ivy.

'Now I appear to you because at last
I have rejoined you for ever. Life has made
Its choice. My affairs are finally quite complete
And there is nothing left in the world to alter.
Whatever you teach will make no difference at all.'

So saying, it boyishly scissored the stone sill
With a careless stretch of the arms and a hint of flannel
As the bells in the tower tensed to tell three quarters
And the moon behaved as it likes to do at these moments,
Nodding above the treescape like an impresario.

Which way it went I really couldn't say,
But it had gone. And so I slowly continued
My right-angled path through the heart of the college,
Less light of foot, but somewhat enlightened,
Slightly unsure of what I thought I had heard.

Darkness was all around me like a sixth
Sense, or the absolute quiet of certain music
That the hand trembles to play. And it was like
The world pressing on its pockets of resistance.
Like righteous claims of love. Or threats of war.

And indeed, I thought, the ultimate chaos will surely be
A predicate of just this irresponsible architecture
Of convinced laws and prayers that meddled for years
With the best of fateful intentions until the wind changed.
The words were in my head like an egg in a bottle.

Thoughts too late to unthink: I had the feeling
Of being betrayed by something of my choosing,
Something I had connived at, something belonging
To the projection of a long-suspected failing,
Haunted by the forces it exploits.